Arseniy Zhilyaev

Museum of Proletarian Culture
The Industrialization of Bohemia

Marsilio

The publication was conceived
as a reflection upon the exhibition
Museum of Proletarian Culture.
The Industrialization of Bohemia

held in
July 12 - September 9, 2012

at the
Tretyakov State Gallery, Moscow

curated by
Kirill Svetlyakov

V-A-C Foundation
Olsufievsky per. 8 bld. 2
Russia Moscow 119021
v-a-c.ru

Arseniy Zhilyaev would like to thank
Nikolay Alekseev, Eugeniy Antufiev, Thomas Campbell,
Maria Chehonadskih, Katerina Chuchalina, Ivan Gorshkov,
Ulya Hashem, Teresa Iarocci Mavica, Martina Mian,
Modern Art Department of Tretyakov State Gallery,
Katya Morozova, NOVATEK, Alexandra Novozhenova,
Dmitry Potemkin, Anastasia Potemkina, Sasha Povzner,
Katya Shuikova, Kirill Svetlyakov, Elena Zaitceva.

Graphic project and editing
Studio Polo 1116, Brugiolo Romanelli, Venezia

First edition May 2013
ISBN 978-88-317-1635

Contents

Museum of Proletarian Culture

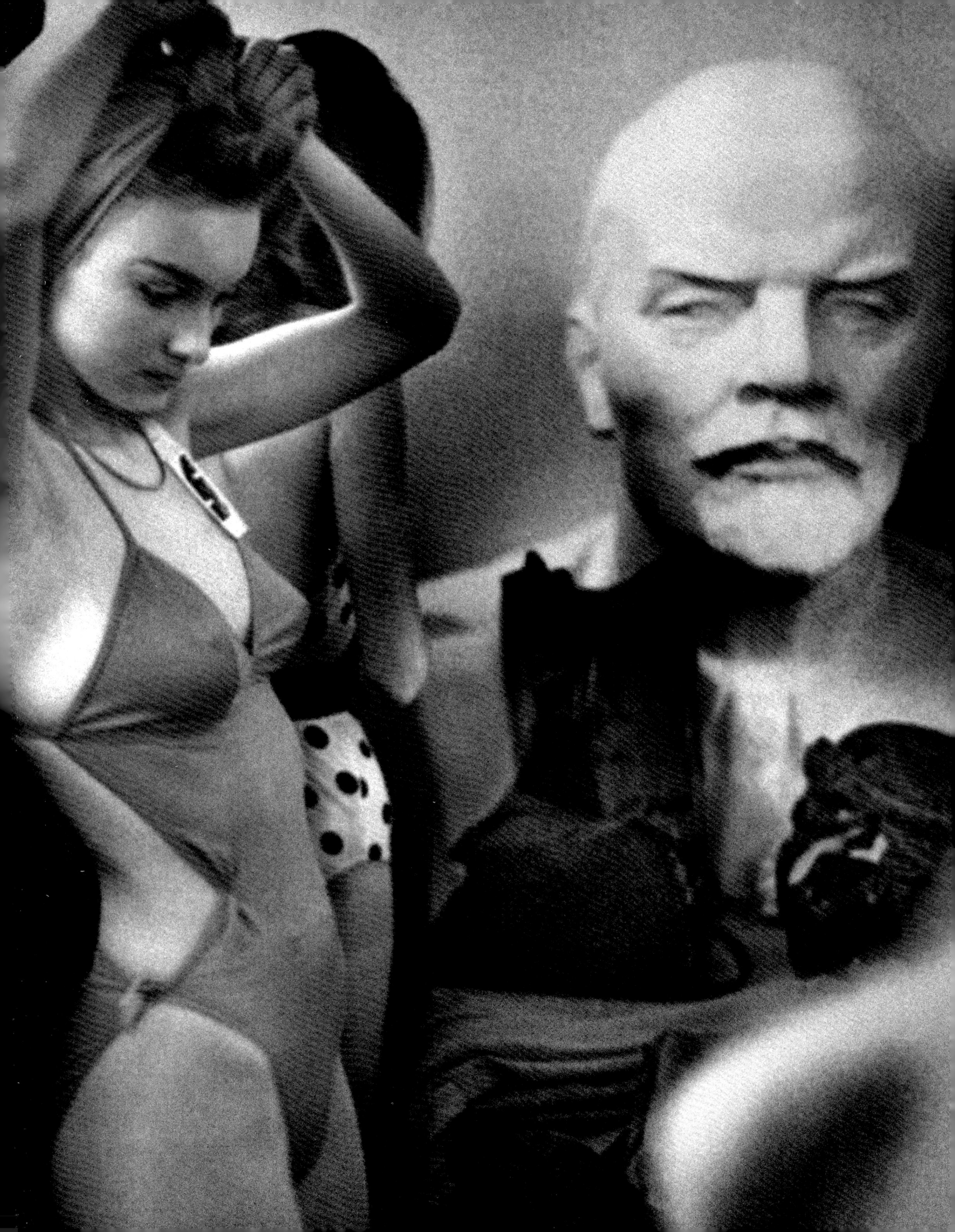

Arseniy Zhilyaev: The Museum as Medium

Nicholas Cullinan

In the summer of 2012, I visited, as I have many times before, the Tretyakov State Gallery in Moscow. Walking around the galleries of the building - itself a repurposed and somewhat threadbare relic of the Soviet era - is both an

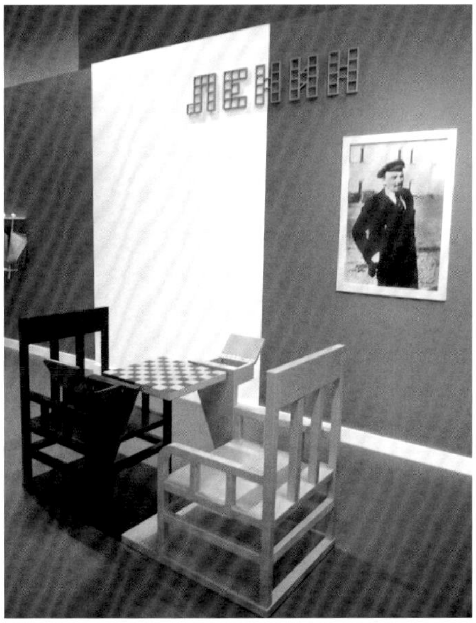

inspiring and a depressing experience, one that provides a fairly accurate but not always flattering mirror to the tumultuous and often tragic history and artistic trajectory of Russian during the twentieth century. The suits of galleries begin as the early twentieth century did - with the enervating experiments and seemingly boundless energy and invention of the Russian avant-garde - the great canvasses and constructions of Natalia Goncharova, Wassily Kandinsky, El Lissitsky, Mikhail Larionov, Liubov Popova, Olga Rozanova, Vladimir Tatlin and Kazimir Malevich. Among these are also reconstructions - not just of lost works, such as Tatlin's counter reliefs, but also of some of the great revolutionary exhibitions, such as the third OBMOKhU exhibition that took place in Moscow in 1921 and at which Alexander Rodchenko's constructions took pride of place, but also another display which reconstructs the heady mix of utopianism and utilitarianism advocated by Russian Constructivist avant-garde designs, as manifested in Rodchenko's plans for a Workers' Club, exhibited at the Exposition Internationale des Arts Décoratifs et Industriels Modernes in Paris in 1925, which was intended to demonstrate the Soviet Union's socially egalitarian and culturally progressive nature to an international audience.

It's downhill from there, as Stalin enters the scene, and the restrictions he placed on art and culture begin to make themselves apparent. The next run of galleries, spanning the period from the 1920s until the 1960s and the emergence of unofficial and nonconformist art, is essentially comprised of Soviet socialist realism, which, with the exception of the more imaginative compositions of figures such as Aleksandr Deineka is mostly comprised of the more earnest and increasingly literal paintings of figures such as Isaak Brodsky, Aleksandr Gerasimov, Yury Pimenov, Kilment Redko, David Shterenberg and Aleksandr Tyshler. Things pick up again

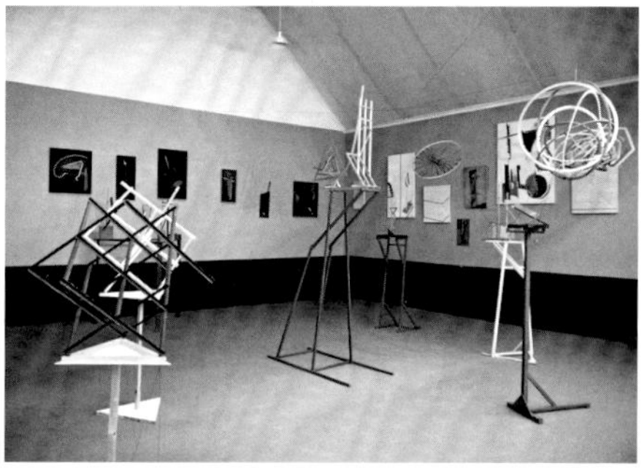

in the run of galleries devoted to Soviet Nonconformist Art, which covers the period from 1953-1986 (after the death of Joseph Stalin and until the advent of Perestroika and Glasnost) and describes work produced outside the aesthetic and ideological constraints of Socialist Realism.

Arseniy Zhilyaev, one of the most interesting and promising young Russian artists working today, fashioned a powerful coda to all of this artistic, political and social heritage, one which telescoped its insightful critique onto the specific history of the very museum in which it was staged, and which the visitor to the Tretyakov encountered in the final gallery of the museum. Through the inclusion of an eclectic and wide-ranging array

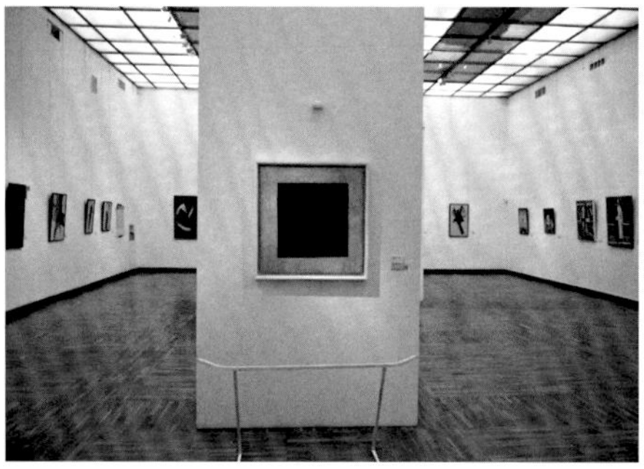

of artefacts, Zhilyaev examined the series of shifts in Russian art over the last three decades, spanning the production of amateur art from the late Soviet years, via the commodification of culture in the post-communist period, and on to the emancipatory and proliferating forms of self-expressions witnessed by today's global social media. As Silvia Franceschini writes: "Bringing together in a single installation a selection of Soviet Realist paintings from the 1920s and 30s, artworks attributed to fictional amateur artists of the latter-day Soviet era and examples of today's shared digital creativity, the project vindicated the value of marginalised and informal creative practices."[1] Zhilyaev is also of course engaging in the "aesthetic of administration," as Benjamin Buchloh has written of the practices of Western conceptual artists such as Mel Bochner and Robert Morris, albeit from an explicitly post-Communist position.[2]

His installation *Museum of Proletarian Culture. The Industrialization of Bohemia* was a response to Alexei Fedorov-Davydov's radical *Experimental Complex Marxist Exhibition* which also took place at the Tretyakov State Gallery in 1931. As Zhilyaev observes: "Arguably nearly 50 years ahead of his time, Fedorov-Davydov tried to show the art of the oppressed to problematise the way art history was, and still is, traditionally taught - as that of the great masters. Placing artworks by a range of celebrated and unknown artists from different eras in the interiors that would have been typically occupied by their owners (such as landowners, merchants or tsars), Fedorov-Davydov's exhibition can be seen as a pioneering installation that aimed to give form to an alternative construction of history - in this instance, a Marxist reading of the history of art that was at odds with the Stalinist promulgation of Socialist Realism as the only officially accepted art form. I was moved by this impulse to articulate an alternative history of art, not based on the celebration of individual creativity but on the relationship between art and the relations of production of its time. Can we subject the history of art to revision today? What would it look like from the point of view of a factory worker of the 1970s or 1980s? And what about the perspective of

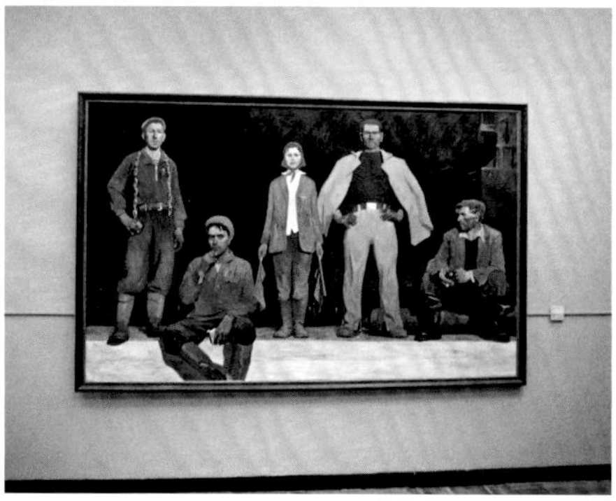

a producer of immaterial goods of the 2000s?"[3]

This palimpsest of specific moments in cultural production and shifting class dynamics was made manifest in Zhilyaev's installation through a nuanced but immediate and discursive display of disparate artefects. These included different typologies and modes of display such as an entire wall dedicated to the early twentieth century Kazakh poet and activist Abay Kunanbaev who not only fostered politically progressive views on Kazakh culture, Islam and the role of women within Kazakh society, but also gave his name to the Occupy Abay move-

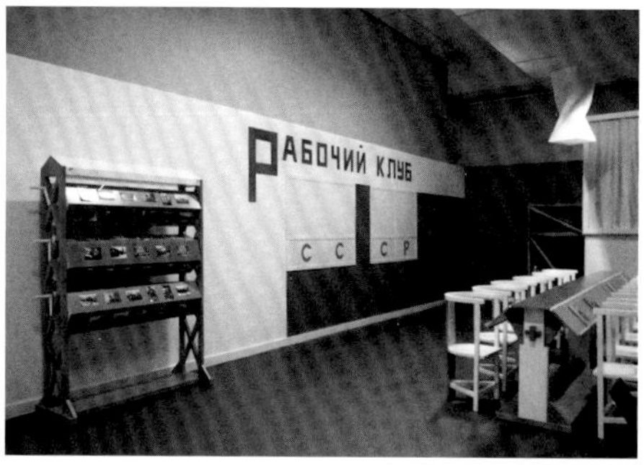

ment, which is the Moscow manifestation of the Occupy movement and which derives it name from its proximity to the monument in Moscow dedicated to Abay Kunanbaev. Elsewhere in Zhilyaev's subtle and thought-provoking curatorial gesture were Soviet workers' collages from the 1970s and 1980s and a fascinating display of home shelving units from the 1990s, which delineated the changing nature of the relationship between work and leisure in post-communist Russia, as the former centres of Soviet amateur (in both senses of the word) artistic engagements, such as Houses of Culture, Pioneer Palaces, Houses of Artists etc., where people had enjoyed engaging in making art after work, were closed down or repurposed for other means and aims. As Zhilyaev comments on this period known as "The Era of Stagnation" from the 1970s and 1980s: "This time of severe political repression, when almost all the undertakings of the 1960s

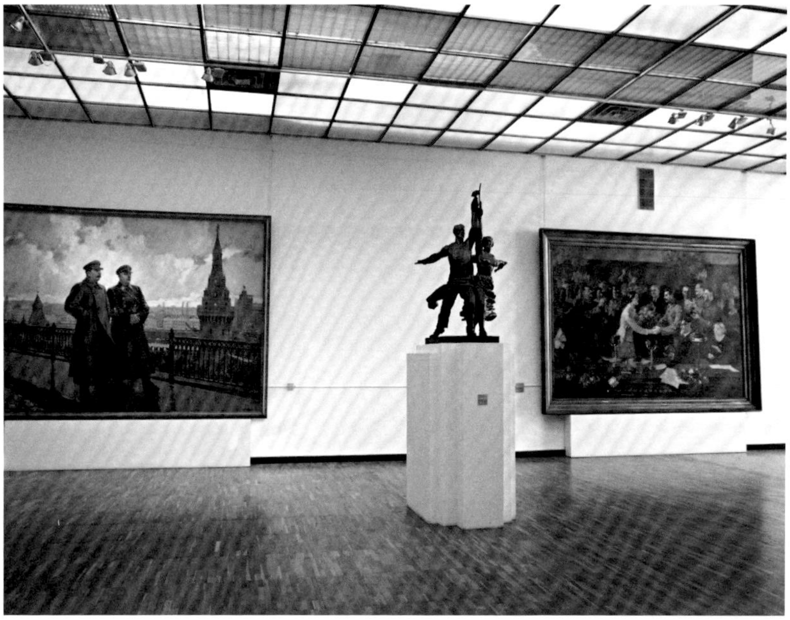

had been discontinued, paradoxically saw the emergence of great art movements such as the Moscow conceptual school. In the late 1970s, one of the only answers to the everyday feeling of hopelessness and timelessness was to express oneself creatively. It was during that period that workers' amateur creativity flourished, exemplified in techniques such as wood-carving, hammered ironwork or amateur furniture design. The strict division between work and leisure during the era of late socialism made this creativity possible. It was an extremely democratic art and this is what still inspires me today."[4]
Finally, Zhilyaev's installation was rounded out by the inclusion of sculptures of Stepan Vasilevich Lugovoi, who made many public statues and works of art during Soviet times and who was represented in Zhilyaev's installation through one of his earliest sculptures of a blacksmith, an embodiment of the Soviet work ethic and social subject.
Zhilyaev's installation *Museum of Proletarian Culture. The Industrialization of Bohemia* at the Tretyakov State Gallery chimes with other projects he has initiated in historically resonant sites in Moscow over the last couple of years. These include the 2012 project *Pedagogical Poem*, made in collaboration with the historian and activist Ilya Budraytskis and staged at the Presnya Historical Memorial Museum, formerly the Museum of Revolution, and which was formed not just by a physical exhibition but, more importantly, by a series of lectures and discussions over an eight month period attended by a diverse range of students, activists, historians and members of the general public. This in turn led to the exhibition *The Archive of the Future Museum of History*, also at the Presnya Historical Memorial Museum in Moscow. As Zhilyaev observes: "It is important to us that Pedagogical Poem takes place in the former Museum of Revolution because our purpose is to rethink the museum as an educational institution connecting history and art and addressed to the wider public. This differs significantly from both the anti-institutional impulse of the Occupy movement and bureau cratized contemporary art academia."[5]
Zhilyaev's interventions in such museums can of course be considered within the more international trajectory of so-called "Institutional Critique", as exemplified by the work of a diverse range of artists from different generations, from Michael Asher, Marcel Broodthaers, Daniel Buren, Andrea Fraser, Fred Wilson, and Hans Haacke, which foregrounds the invisible machinations of the art institution. But Zhilyaev updates this discussion to the digital era, and the way in which André Malraux's concept of the "musée imaginaire" has been updated to the age of social media and the way in which the idea of curating your own "wall" on sites such as Facebook has proliferated so wildly and internationally, and which of course flags up the current ubiquity of the term "curator" and the way in which social media has proliferated a version of Joseph Beuys' maxim that everyone is an artist. In this, Zhilyaeav has achieved an unusually complex and subtle layering of time and place, as we move from the specificity of Soviet culture spanning the twentieth-century, into the disembodied digital world of today.

[1] http://www.afterall.org/online/artists-at-work-arseniy-zhilyaev.
[2] Benjamin H.D. Buchloh, *Conceptual Art 1962-1969. From the Aesthetic of Administration to the Critique of Institutions*, in *October* 55, Winter 1990, pp. 105-143.
[3] http://www.afterall.org/online/artists-at-work-arseniy-zhilyaev.
[4] *Ibid.*
[5] *Ibid.*

Arseniy Zhilyaev's Museum of Proletarian Culture and the Politics of Art Museums Today

Kirill Svetlyakov

The debate around art museums started from the moment they were established. The curators of the Louvre argued that the historical principle of exhibiting artworks diminishes their aesthetic value: history kills art. German museums, meanwhile, offered their alternative: by exhibiting the history of stylistic periods through plaster cast reproductions. In turn, the former royal collections practiced the aesthetic cult of geniuses and masterpieces which have their origins in Romanticism and still exist to this day despite iconoclastic practices during the 20th century. It is all very simple: the "geniuses" and the "masterpieces" sell more easily on the marketplace and in the museum where the viewer, feeling that they have been at one with the masterpiece, proceeds to the museum's shop to get that masterpiece in the form of a poster, a t-shirt, a magnet etc. At present, the souvenir store has become a direct extension of the museum exhibition.

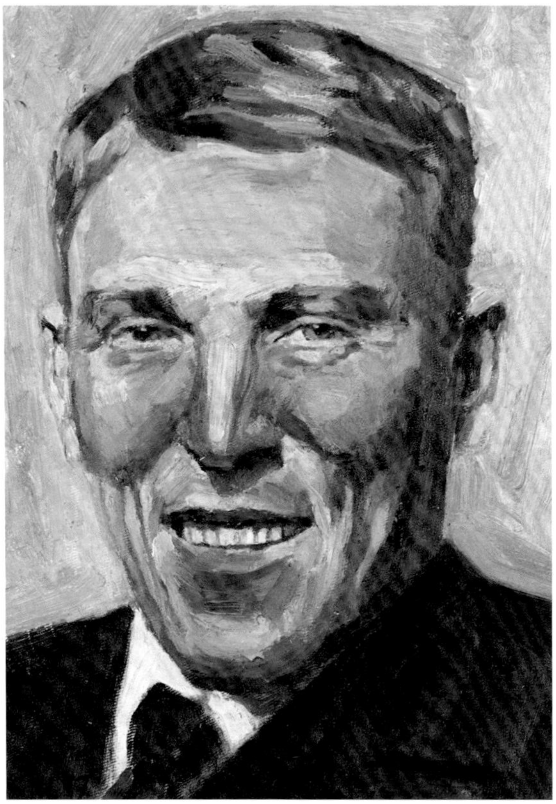

Up to this day, museum employees, and particularly those at the Tretyakov State Gallery, share this "aesthetic taste" approach towards works of art, which was typical of the latter-day Soviet liberal intelligentsia, wallowing in commercial fetishism. This approach, petty-bourgeois to its core, forces museum curators to position every work of art as if it is a potential or actual masterpiece. But here is a problem: the masterpieces "don't work" and aren't recognized as such. That is because the "purely artistic" qualities the members of the liberal intelligentsia love talking about are a pure myth in relation to the second half of the 20th century, when artistic production lost its stable characteristics and became situational and procedural. That is why the "severe style" of artistic production is impossible to picture outside of the context of the youth, theme-based or "Danish" exhibitions of the 1960s, and the production of the "Sixties" ("Shestidesiatniki") generation – non-conformist art is impossible to introduce separately from the formation of the "shadow" art market and the alternative ways of art consumption that were around.

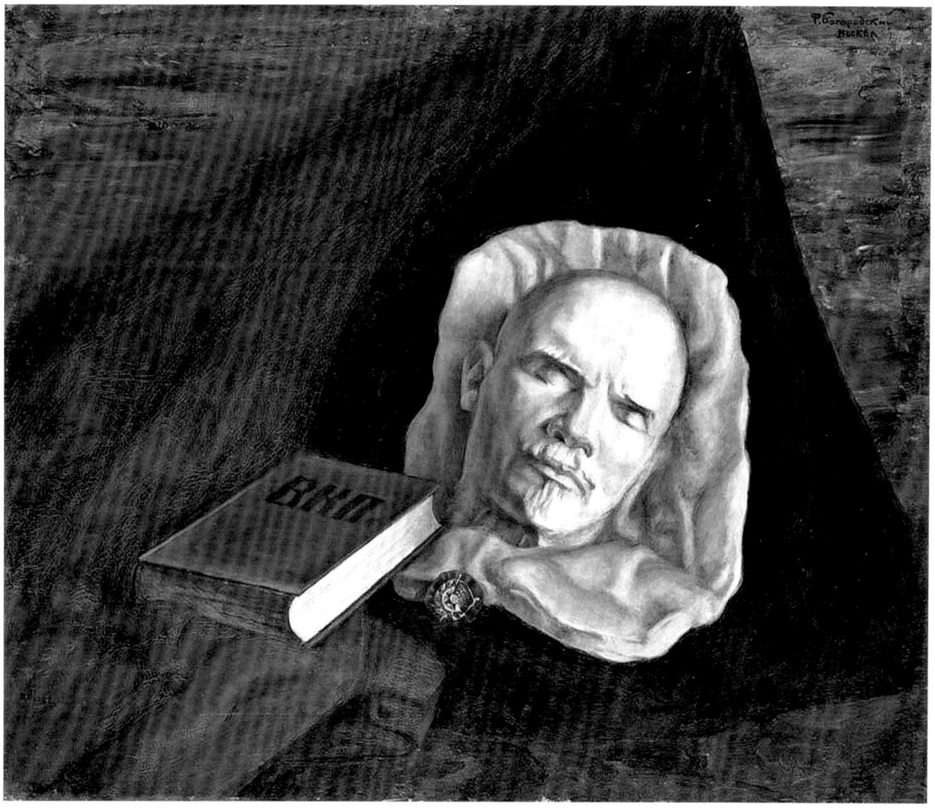

Many of the leading critics nowadays love discussing artistic process as a transition from the production of objects to the production of events. Such thoughts are positioned and perceived as a modern viewpoint even though they first emerged not even in the 1960s but in the 1920s. So, in 1929, in the *Press and Revolution* journal, Alexei Fedorov-Davydov published his article called *The Principles of Building Art Museums* which has not lost any of its topicality in spite of the disappearance of the proletariat in the class interpretation and the dominance of neoliberalism in the contemporary situation. In his article, Fedorov-Davydov criticizes the commercial fetishism of the Soviet museums which, in his words, can be explained through the private-ownership origins of the majority of the museum's collections: "When we summarise the critique of our art museums' exhibitions, we reach the sad conclusion that they exhibit not the true process of artistic evolution but rather a fictitious one; that the art is presented here in a subjective, narrow, bourgeois, idealistic light. They preach that the bourgeois art of classical painting is the one and only true, distinguished and outstanding art form. Semi-classical or industrial art is presented from the perspective of classical art, and, moreover, from the viewpoint of the highest level of establishing these principles in the decadent ideology of art for art's sake."[1]

Of course, contemporary bour-

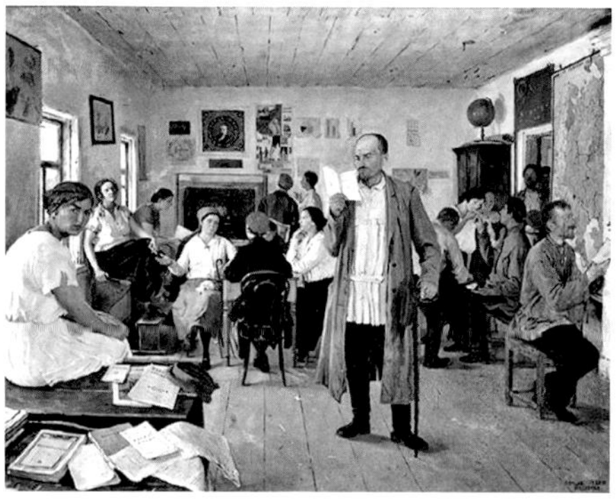

geois museums don't exhibit only paintings; nevertheless, the commercial fetishism keeps on growing with the growth of the new private museums and collections where every object is positioned primarily as "mine," as private property which is served by the curators and the critics.

As an alternative to the bourgeois approach towards museum management, Fedorov-Davydov suggests "displaying not objects but processes. The history of styles stretched in the single straight line of evolution is, for us, a prejudice we have already overcome. We know that this single line does not exist, that each segment of the historical process is a complicated interlay, a dialectic struggle between forces and tendencies of different types and different focuses."[2]

The method of functional exhibitionism suggested by Fedorov-Davydov presupposes a contrast between different cultural phenomena which make it possible to view the works of art from the widest possible angle – from a social phenomenon to a fact of art and everyday life.

At present, such experiments sometimes happen at exhibitions but they have a very limited influence on overcoming the traditional museums' static and monumental nature.

The project of Arseniy Zhilyaev's

Museum of Proletarian Culture has been carried out within the framework of the *Artist and His Museum* program and features works of art created by the artist himself as well as everyday objects he has found around former Soviet enterprises and workers' clubs. This is a kind of an experimental model of a museum which has broken its ties with the commercial fetishism of the ordinary museums as well as of the neoliberal museums of modern art which are rapidly transforming themselves into recreational, entertainment, and shopping centers.

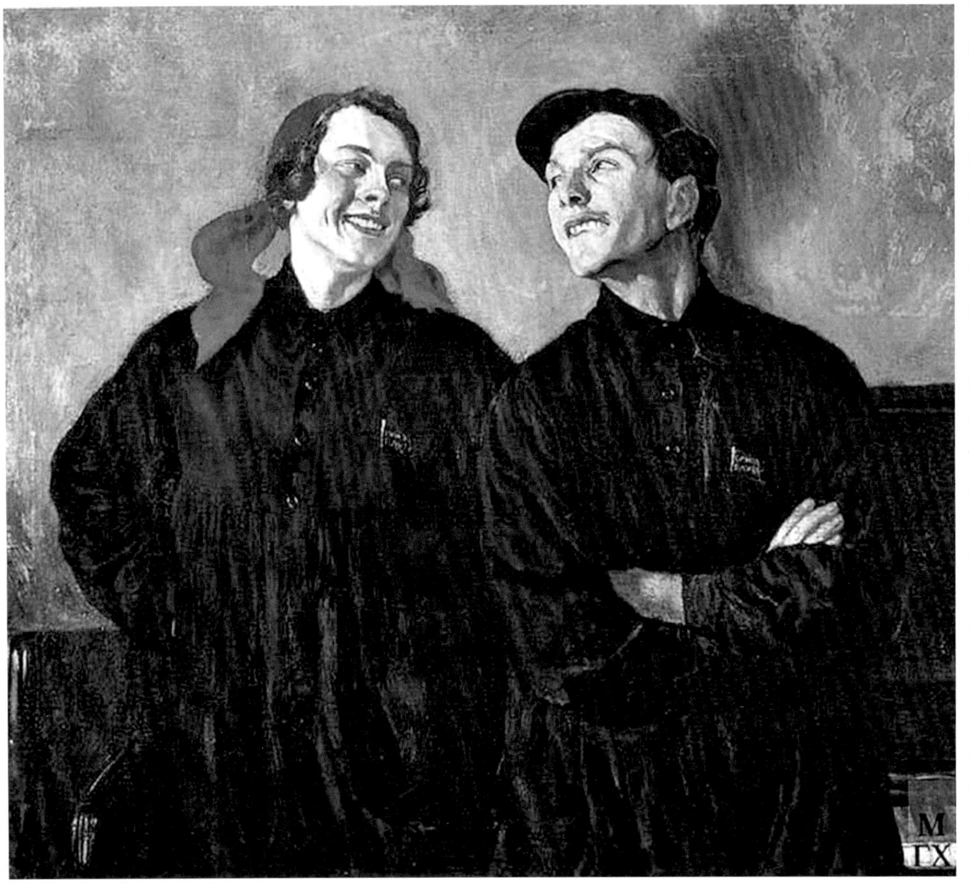

In Fedorov-Davydov's time, proletarian culture was being designed as an alternative to bourgeois culture but the alternative never actually materialized because as early as the 1930s, radical and dynamic Communist culture gave way to the static "Palace" culture and the access of the masses to the cultural achievements of the former ruling classes and societal segments. At the same time, the art of the masses' was presented as the foundation of proletarian culture, but existed only within the framework of the traditional cultural hierarchies of the distinguished and grass-roots artistic movements. Among the proletarian culture's achievements, special attention should be given to the legendary educational institution ZNUI (People's Correspondence University of the Arts) which outstrips all western mail-art practices and attempts at finding the aesthetics of interaction.

Within the framework of his project, Zhilyaev creates a rather idealized model of the proletarian museum partially resembling a memorial complex, which seemingly contradicts Fedorov-Davydov's directives. Every work of art and every object in this complex is aimed at exposing and representing the social processes transpiring in the latter-day Soviet and post-Soviet society. Zhilyaev begins the conversation about modern art with the issue of the heroes of labor and the contemporary labor relations which determine the means of artistic production.

In 1931, the Tretyakov State Gallery exhibition organized by Fedorov-Davydov on a social-class principle was subjected to criticism for its attempt at combining art and everyday life and for its simplified, vulgar sociological approach to exhibiting material. The author himself thought of his exhibition as a social study – one of many potentially possible ones. To an extent, such studies have heralded the emergence of installations created on the basis of documentary materials.

At the present time, the debates over whether historical documentary exhibitions kill art or not are no longer topical, because history is often the only condition for the creation and existence of works of art despite the fictional stories created around commercial fetishes.

[1] Alexei Fedorov-Davydov, *Principles of Art Museum Development*, in A. Fedorov-Davydov, *Russian and Soviet Art. Articles and Essays*, Moscow 1975, p. 115.

[2] *Ibid.*

The Museum of Proletarian Culture. The Industrialization of Bohemia

Maria Chekhonadskih

Should We End the Project of Institutional Critique or Begin It Again?

In their novels, the first utopians described a new type of institution, accessible to every single citizen, combining library, exhibition space, lecture hall, and workshops. The museum – a distant relative of Campanella's *City of the Sun* – was conceived as a public space where knowledge production would emerge through cooperation and communication among free citizens. This new project was the antithesis of the private galleries where aristocrats kept their art collections of art and their chambers of curiosities. Art was supposed to move out of the palaces and residences of kings and into the public space.

This model evolved over a long period during which the Enlightenment narrowed the distance between utopian conceptions of the future and the real world through pragmatic reform and architecture, developing the idea of social institutions and their special responsibility to society. The museum's emancipatory purpose was to establish a better life here on earth. Nothing has remained of the idea of utopia, however, except for an enthusiasm for publicity,

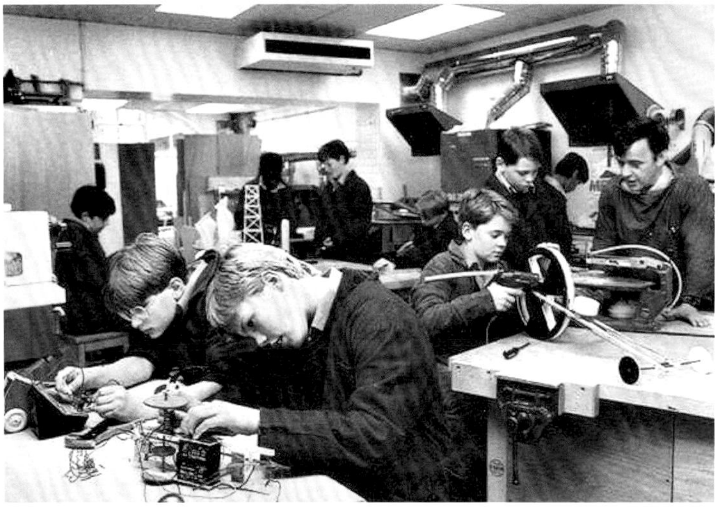

and the projects that were realized quite soon became places of recreation and relaxation for wealthy citizens. Artistic milestones have been preserved in the museum, and it has been the past that has been more on display there, with the future no longer mentioned. Having become a heaven on earth in the shape of a secularized temple of the arts, the museum has abandoned its utopian role.[1]

Indeed, the museum has turned into an urban resort: it supplies viewers with a cultural leisure service and a staff to serve their needs – artists with their works, art historians with their texts, and curators with their exhibitions. After gaining autonomy, an institution originally created by artists and philosophers has given birth to artists and philosophers who service the institution.[2] Thus, the museum has become a place for reproducing dogmas, hierarchies, and systems of established relationships, which are exactly what museum exhibits are supposed to tell us about.

In the nineteen-seventies, a flurry of institutional critique descended on museums as vehicles of power's bureaucratic and repressive apparatus. The sprawling assemblage of institutions had not only concocted a tangled web of mediations between various actors in the same chain – between artist and curator, curator and museum management, museum management and society, and, finally, between society and artist. It was also a clear expression of the Fordist project as a whole, of the disciplinary society and assembly line routine, which blocked freedom of thought, spontaneous behavior, and creative ini-

tiative, plunging culture and the social imaginary into the abyss of reproduction, consumption, and alienation.
It would be no exaggeration to say that the institutional critique that took shape in western theory and art history in the seventies had common roots with the anti-bureaucratic fervor of Soviet intellectuals and dissidents, who, although they could not openly attack the Brezhnev era's "all-meetinged-out" bureaucrats, actively expressed their hatred of the power apparatuses established in late Soviet society, identifying themselves as enemies of the "authoritarian regime."[3] Artists elaborated their critique of Soviet behavioral norms and lifestyles by escaping or deconstructing cliché semi-official language, creating informal communities and circles, and inventing their own

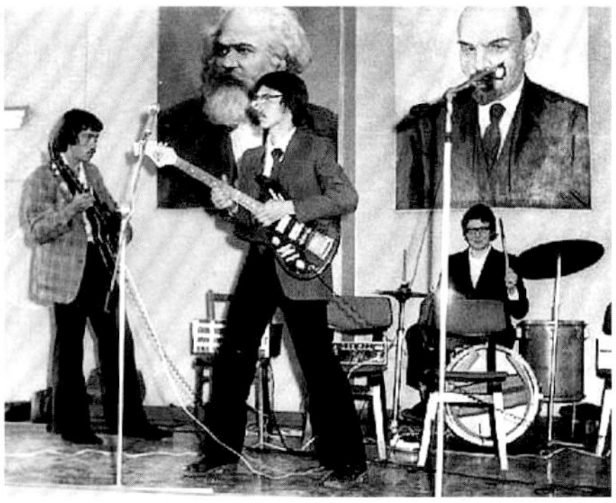

lexicons and secret terms, whose mastery marked participants as belonging to a particular group of kindred spirits. Soviet anti-bureaucratic and anti-authoritarian fervor resulted in the massive exodus of progressive intellectuals and artists from public cultural institutions during the post-Soviet era. They preferred new, informal initiatives, based on self-organization and entrepreneurship, to the old, monstrous institutions, which were unamenable to reform.
Whereas during the first two post-Soviet decades institutional

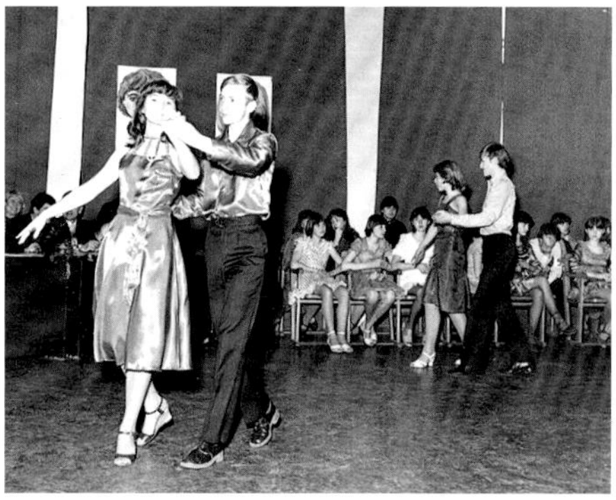

critique drowned in the new pro-market euphoria, and abandoned, forgotten cultural institutions were shunted from progressive society's field of view, analysis of unresolved institutional issues has today become a necessity, as past traumas have the tendency to come back in the shape of the real, as new authoritative and political establishments, whose subjects are often the selfsame critics of the "old" bureaucracy.
While the old regime's museums were forgotten and abandoned, they filled up with various business projects and creative managerial exhibitions, which aggressively recycled the contents of these institutions into attractive forms of entertainment. A number of Soviet museums and exhibition complexes were reduced to ruins due to a lack of financing and continued their operations mechanically, fighting for survival in the new reality more than anything else. The Soviet legacy was either repressed and sent straight to the dump at the behest of the new cultural entrepreneurs, adapted to the needs of the tourism business or assessed in the light of "democracy," "the market," and "liberal values." Former teachers of Marxism-Leninism, who quickly adopted the new clichéd language of market ideology, often implemented this revaluation of values. The old regime's institutions thus preserved the old forms of life, having merely purged socialist rhetoric from the language of the nomenklatura management style. An allergy to all forms of official culture occluded the possibility of constructively critiquing the old institutions. However, the relics of the Soviet legacy and the set of problems that gave rise to them could not disappear by themselves, and so today, like ruins of the past, they come to life in the shape of cartoonish departments, new ideological departments, and committees for the defense of morality.
Arseny Zhilyaev's project *Museum of Proletarian Culture. The Industrialization of Bohemia* has appeared amidst a new round in public debates on the destiny and role of old cultural institutions, a round marked by the emergence of an alternative political and ethical attitude to the Soviet project that is bereft of "hysterical sighing" and emotional reactions. Breaking the taboo on all things Soviet and trying to pull it out of the ghetto-cum-zoo of tourist "creativity," Zhilyaev attempts to analyze the past's institutional vicissitudes and understand what our new future might be like if we examine the Soviet project in all its multidimensionality and complexity. Opening up new areas of potentiality in the avant-garde objectives of sixties-era Soviet modernism, on the one hand, and the complex dialectic of the struggle amongst

various tendencies within institutions, on the other, Zhilyaev enters an old museum in order to present his research in the shape of a fictional museum of the future.

A Fictional Museum

The exhibition *Museum of Proletarian Culture. The Industrialization of Bohemia* was held at the branch of the Tretyakov State Gallery specializing in twentieth-century art. In creating his own museum within the museum, Zhilyaev turns to its archive in order to research exhibition practices in the thirties and the history of Soviet modernist architecture in the sixties. Zhilyaev enters the museum through the back door, paying attention to the design of the Soviet museum and exposing its architectonics, which was meant to support specific mechanisms of knowledge production.

Zhilyaev's objective coincides with the line of critiquing outmoded forms of museum work, while his research of displaced and marginal types of creativity suggests an alternative viewpoint on art practices. In other words, the core of the *Museum of Proletarian Culture. The Industrialization of Bohemia* is the complex dialectic between museum and artist. How and under what conditions does an artist end up in a museum? When and why do artists engage in artistic creation outside the museum? Are museums the spaces where the "event" of art takes place? What does founding a museum mean, and who founds it? Do museums make it possible to change our future? And who is the subject of this change? Zhilyaev believes the answer to this question can be found in the history of the oppressed, of those people whose art has been shown and preserved outside museums. This perspective gives rise to a complex study in which an analysis of museums as institutions and a genealogical analysis of folk art merge.

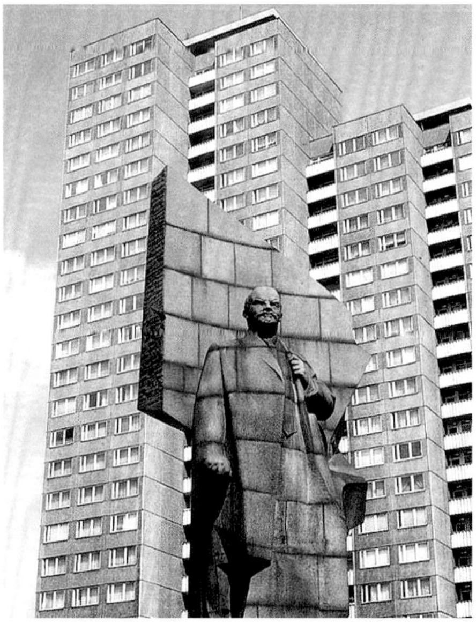

In addition, the *Museum of Proletarian Culture. The Industrialization of Bohemia* is a conceptual response to Alexei Fedorov-Davydov's *Experimental Marxist Exhibition*, which opened at the Tretyakov State Gallery in 1931. For the first time on the institutional level, viewers were shown the art of oppressed classes. And whereas at the time the exhibition was criticized for its vulgar determinism, since art was shown to be wholly dependent on its social and economic context, over half a century later, Fedorov-Davydov's innovative approach has been appreciated and reinterpreted.

In the didactic exhibition model, items are presented not as free-standing objects or autonomous artworks, but as phenomena from a single chain of causes and effects. Fedorov-Davydov began developing this way of showing art in the late twenties: its aim was to destroy the bourgeois logic of autonomous works, isolated and highlighted on the white walls of the gallery (the so-called white cube). The didactic exhibition and the corresponding principle of contextualizing art highlight the

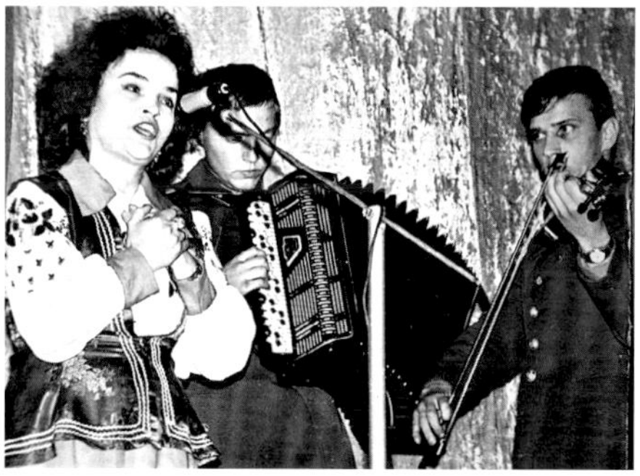

historical and social backgrounds of works by adding accompanying texts, artifacts, and historical documents, as well as by grouping works in a particular way so as to liberate them as much as possible from fetishization, that is, by exposing the hidden logic of the historical processes underlying particular stylistic and formal features of the works, and, as a radical invariant, by revealing the relations of production. Fedorov-Davydov thus set out to show the historical process in its entirety by means of a museum narrative that could be partly based on works of applied and decorative art that had been displaced from art history.[4]

Zhilyaev suggests once again raising the issue of the relationship between aesthetics and the conditions of artistic production, enhanced in his project by an analysis of history and the political context. This analysis, however, is diametrically opposed to the strictly academic approach taken by the museum curator Fedorov-Davydov. For Zhilyaev, the museum is primarily a medium enabling him to deconstruct institutional politics as such. The exhibition thus becomes a total installation where it is impossible to distinguish architecture from assemblage, fact from fiction, document from literature. Zhilyaev partially imitates and partially appropriates elements of Soviet interiors, with their typical stands and flowers in planters, showing his preference for a linear historical chronology, simplification of the material, visual impact, and instructiveness, in order to generate a particular atmosphere and link his imaginary museum with the real museum in which his exhibition unfolds.

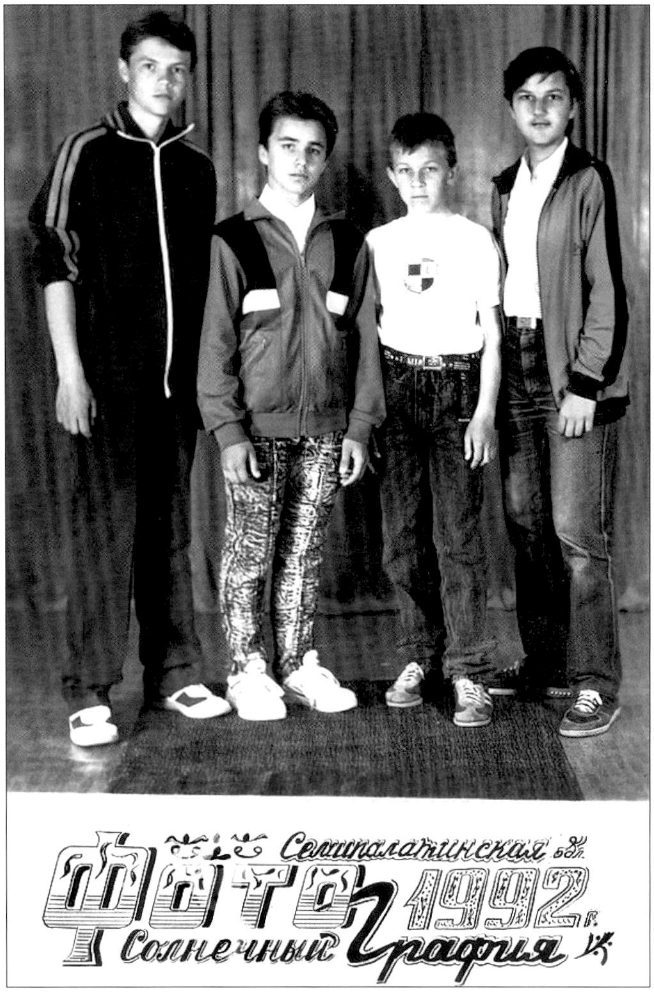

Indeed, viewers here find themselves as it were in the era of didactic exhibitions. First, the late Soviet period unfolds before them: its protagonists are workers, engineers, and amateur artists. This then gives way to the history of the creative class during the almost-futuristic nineties and noughties. Viewers realize, however, that they are in a museum within the museum, and so the conventionality and literariness of the proceedings is a pivotal aspect of their experience. It is a fictional museum, populated by characters rather than real historical figures. Their works are subjected to conjecture, reconstruction, and, finally, "retrospective" inscription into the history of proletarian art by the artistic imagination of the exhibition's creator.

Zhilyaev does not select works of folk art in the manner of an anthropologist collecting artifacts, like the curator Fedorov-Davydov or, to invoke a more recent example, the artist Jeremy Deller. Rather, he "conceptualizes" phenomena of Soviet self-made design, the various late-Soviet craft items made by workers, and artifacts of today's media culture in order to tell an alternative history of art. Assuming that the rejection of autonomous art, which was imbricated in the logic of the Soviet avant-garde and expressed in the utopian appeal to fuse art and life, was continued in the leisure activities of workers and the technical intelligentsia, Zhilyaev revisits species of spontaneous creativity, giving them the status of an avant-garde that evolved in parallel with official art. Here, the artistic imagination substantiates the research undertaken by Zhilyaev, and thus his "folk avant-garde" is more of a conceptual invention, a part of the fictional museum that constitutes the shapes of the social and political imagination.

Telling Stories: Document and Readymade

The official version of events always constitutes our memory, history, and point of view. Point of view can be understood in the literal sense as what is visible and liable to public display. Most Russian museums were repositories of this official representation of history, and this continues today in the guise of the new heroes of post-Soviet reality. Expositions are filled with figures rehabilitated by the new ideology by way of blatantly demonstrating local patriotism. Popular art forms are hardly recorded, because they are not included in official catalogues and archives, and thus cannot be represented in the classical way. Zhilyaev has to work with raw material, pieces of which must be collected into a coherent assemblage of stories. The performativity of his gesture has to do with how he models the "aesthetic" situation. Ultimately, his exhibition is a total installation of anonymous works, reconstructed artifacts, and found objects. He finds the materials he needs on the Internet, in trash dumps and old buildings, and

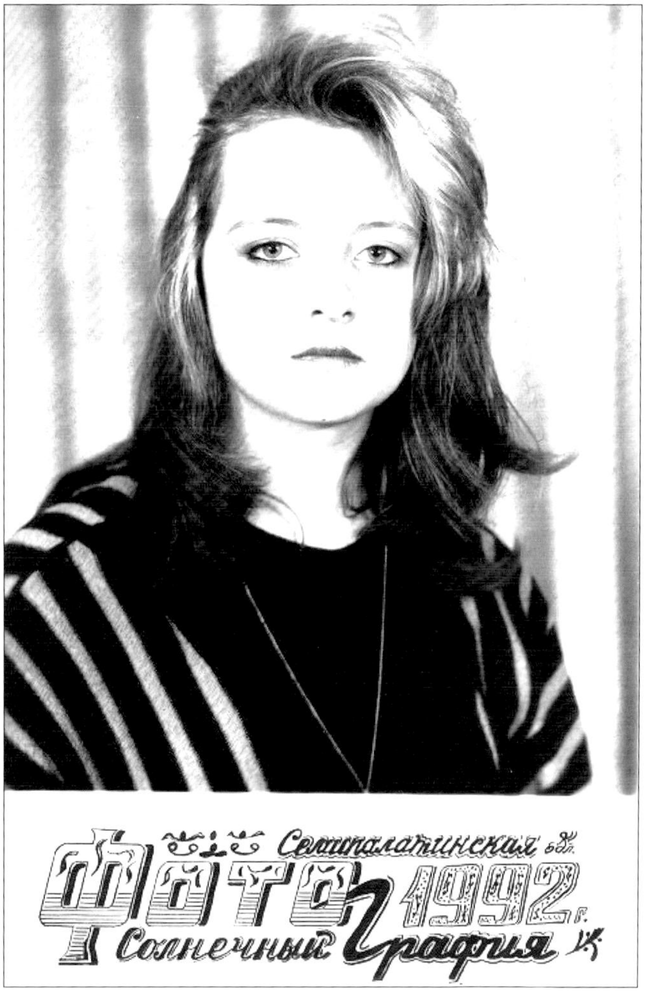

some of the objects he makes himself. In essence, they are all documents and facts of life of the late Soviet and post-Soviet era, but they enter the fictional space of the aesthetic situation thanks to the artist. Assembling these materials into a single expositional whole amounts to a fictional manipulation of the "historical sources." Working on the verge of the documentary and the performative indeed enables Zhilyaev to effectively and convincingly show a fictitious event as real.

The legitimation of popular art undertaken by Zhilyaev is somewhat reminiscent of Kafka's short story *Josephine the Singer, or the Mouse Folk*.[5] The mouse folk are factory workers who suffer deprivations and work hard. Josephine, one of the factory workers, entertains the others with her singing. Having no voice, technique or musical training, Josephine squeaks more than she sings, but it is this piping that fascinates the mouse folk. In Maurizio Lazzarato's reading, Josephine's singing acquires the status of art only because the piping she produces is a kind of readymade: it maintains the status of art while Josephine sings at the factory, but as soon as she demands official recognition as a singer and exemption from her job at the factory, her singing is recognized as piping. At this point, the workers turn away from Josephine and demand she return to work. Similarly, Duchamp's urinal is a work of art only because the artist intellectually construed it as such, while outside of this intellectual construction it remains a urinal.[6]

Zhilyaev's fictional museum operates within the same logic of readymades: his folk avant-garde becomes such within the artist's mental construct. This is not contradicted by the fact that his history of alternative forms of creativity falls into the trap of nineties-era capitalist legitimation. Zhilyaev thus brings Josephine's dream to its absurd conclusion: demanding autonomy, non-professional squeaking can only be a "commercial product." He therefore shows how popular crafts, unrecognized as art, are transformed into an autonomous species of "creative activity" and become a full-fledged part of the post-Soviet capitalist culture industry.

In his project, Zhilyaev contrast two eras – the late Soviet period of work/leisure, at whose dawn independent, anonymous forms of creativity were born, and the post-Soviet era, which professionalized them and raised the "ploughboy artists" to the level of commercial culture. While the museum dictates the rhythms of artistic production, where creativity complies with the institutional machine of societal and political demands, anonymous recreational art is a side effect of this machine, since it was born in amateur art circles, workers' clubs, and houses of culture. Gathered here is an entire ensemble of voices, stories, and documents that reveal the historical vicissitudes of the legitimation of popular art, which emerged independently from the underground of culture and leisure activities into the arena of mass commercial production.

Here we are confronted with the anonymous creators of the late Soviet era – for example, railroad worker Ilya Dondurenko, who dreamed of an era of new high-speed trains and spaceships that would enable people to move around the globe easily and quickly. He laid kilometer after kilometer of railroad ties, and in his leisure time crafted architectural models from matches. His *Model No. 14* is built in the shape of a sickle and hammer crowned with a five-domed church. The maniacal love for fashioning tiny houses from matchboxes, burning portraits and landscapes onto wood, and building shelves and tables amidst the scarcity of Soviet daily life, had only one face and that was the face of a Soviet worker escaping from factory discipline into the realm of "creative leisure," where the dogmas of Soviet ideology passed through the filters of his social experience.

Zhilyaev attempts to show us the features of that face, and that is why there is something Kabakovian about the exposition: the protagonists of this exhibition are partly fictitious, have partly been turned into characters, and have partly themselves become artifacts of Soviet and post-Soviet culture as such. They give way to the cacophony of the experiments of the nineties, when workers' clubs and houses of cultures generated a new pop culture, and creative time, which had been liberated from work, demanded that it be recognized as work. Former workers, engineers, and female vocational school students became musicians, artists, and talk-show hosts, such that new forms of cultural politics and show business emerged in which the culture of the future was forged, and the model of alternative cultural production turned into entrepreneurship. This grassroots culture was privatized by business. This is partly what happened with the institution of contemporary art, which went through an analogous process of emancipation before returning, in the noughties, to the museum. While the creative professions have become the basis of the post-Fordist economy, their scope and idealist fervor have been reduced to working to order. This is exactly what has happened to grassroots forms of spontaneous creativity, which have gradually been transformed into the machine of the culture industry, a process that Andrew Ross has termed the "industrialization of Bohemia."[7]

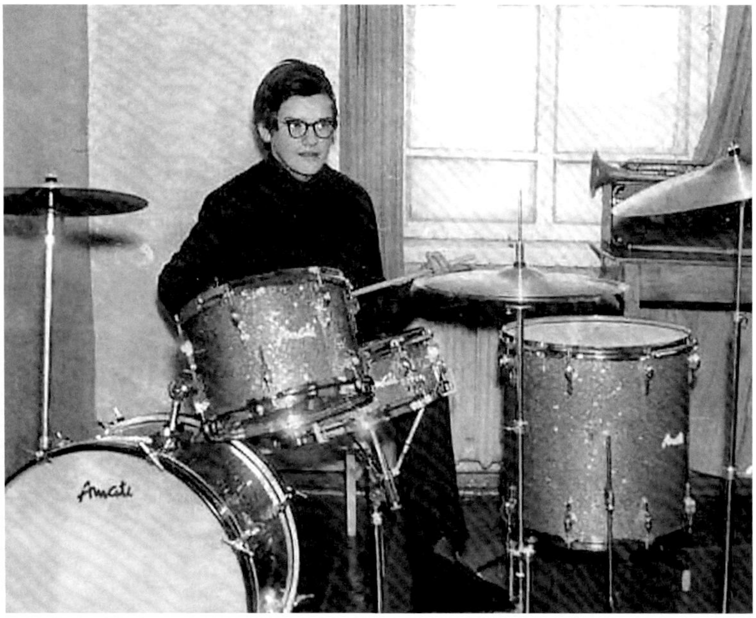

The industrialization of Bohemia began during the days of Warhol's Factory: Warhol showed the importance of the rhythm of mass production and commercial routine. Thirty years later, managers in Silicon Valley took the opposite route: they made business fashionable by imitating patterns of creative work and the bohemian lifestyle. Companies looked for artists who knew web design, and then used their style and creativity to develop an entire industry. Since artists were accustomed to accepting non-monetary forms of compensation, symbolic capital was sufficient payment for their labor: "The combination of this coping mentality with a production code of aesthetic perfectibility is a godsend for managers looking for employees capable of self-discipline under the most extreme job pressure."[8] As a result of this procedure, it was possible to capitalize not only the fruits of labor but also the thoughts, impulses, and emotions of employees. The countercultural community was thus gradually incorporated into the new economy from the late eighties on.[9] By analogy, we could argue that the post-Soviet industrialization of Bohemia began when business arrived in the realm of creativity. Like popular forms of culture, professional art has become part of the entertainment industry landscape.

Zhilyaev's creative class has found new ways of resisting creativity's usurpation by capital. He believes that today the poetry of the multitudes, who are fashioning the idiom of contemporary visual culture in the social networks, might be deemed an incarnation of the folk avant-garde. Analyzing this situation, the expositional narrative approaches its culmination. Despite the industrialization of creativity and the transformation of all and sunder into show business, in the noughties a new emancipatory culture of social network users emerged: the folklore of demotivators, Internet memes, graffiti, texts, photos, and posts has generated a space of free exchange and cooperation among millions of people around the world both inside and outside the Web. A similar type of creativity has grown out o the experience of the new generation of immaterial workers - students, office workers, media workers, and IT specialists. It was just this segment of society who actively participated in the protests in Russia in the winter and spring of 2012, establishing new forms of political life in the process. One such form is the general assembly. According to Zhilyaev, the event of

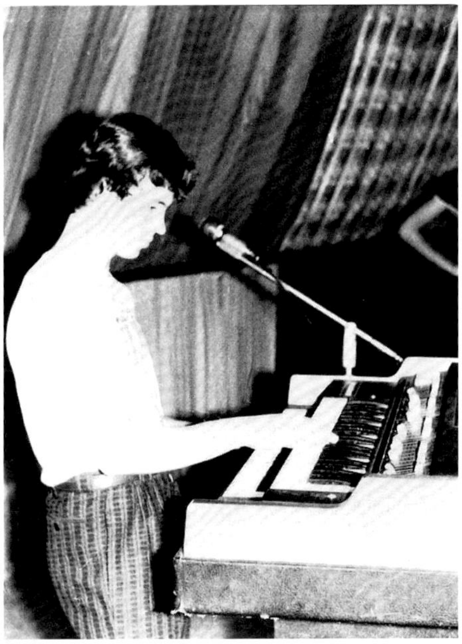

the general assembly heralds a new decade in the twenty-first century. Such is Zhilyaev's response: instead of constituted power (the rule of institutions with their attendant hierarchies and canonical forms of representation) we are faced with the constituent power of the multitudes and the anonymous, who despite everything continue to resist the machinery of power.
The *Museum of Proletarian Culture. The Industrialization of Bohemia* gives no final answers but rather leaves questions open. Who is an artist at this point in history, and what should we call art? What are its functions, and can we speak of the emergence of a new subject who does not conform to the rhythms of the institutional assembly line? The exhibition gives us a perspective on the future with its new forms of creative activity. In this case, the museum ought to become a social center where these forms acquire their new constituent meaning.
At first glance, Zhilyaev's exhibition is far from the classical specimens of institutional critique, as his project is focused on imaginary forms of the future, on revolution and the new revolutionary subject that must replace the working class, which has been destroyed by the market economy, and change society. Zhilyaev finds that this class matured in the workers' clubs of the late-Soviet period. Like the first utopians, he wants to return the spirit of building new forms of social life to the museum. Whereas Francis Bacon saw his museum project as a platform for realizing the ideal city and imaginary communities of the future,[10] Zhilyaev believes that his fictional museum, installed in the body of a great historical art museum, can incite new forms of subjectification on the part of viewers, from reassessing their attitude to the Soviet project to direct mobilization and politicization. Thus, his appeal to the Soviet history of architecture, exhibitions, and exhibition work opens the debate over the possible shapes of institutional critique at the local level and offers a new project of interpreting the Soviet past via the radical revision of institutional mechanisms.

[1] Andrew McClellan, *From Boullée to Bilbao: the museum as utopian space*, in *Art History and Its Institutions: Foundations of a Discipline*, ed. Elizabeth Mansfield, New York & London, Routledge, 2002, pp. 46-64.
[2] Here I am paraphrasing Cornelius Castoriadis, who described, in the seventies, the process by which institutions become autonomous vis-à-vis society: "We are instead thinking of the fact [...] that once an institution is established it seems to become autonomous, the fact that it possesses its own inertia and its own logic, that, in its continuance and in its effects, it outstrips its function, its 'ends,' and its 'reasons for existing.' The apparent plain truths are turned upside-down: what could have been seen 'at the start' as an ensemble of institutions in the service of society becomes a society in the service of institutions." Cornelius Castoriadis, *The Imaginary Institution of Society*, trans. Kathleen Blamey, Cambridge, Mass., MIT Press, 1987, p. 110.
[3] On the similarities between anti-institutionalism in the west and east during the Cold War, see Blake Stimson, *What was institutional critique?*, in *Institutional Critique: An Anthology of Artists' Writings*, ed. Alexander Alberro and Blake Stimson, Cambridge, Mass., MIT Press, 2009, pp. 20-42.
[4] See Alexei Fedorov-Davydov, *Principles of Art Museum Development*, in the present volume.
[5] Franz Kafka, *Josephine the Singer, or the Mouse Folk*, trans. Willa and Edwin Muir, in *The Complete Stories*, New York, Schocken Books, 1971, pp. 360-376.
[6] Maurizio Lazzarato, *Art, Work and Politics in Disciplinary Societies and Societies of Control*, trans. Alberto Toscano, *Radical Philosophy*, no. 149, May-June 2008, pp. 26-32.
[7] Andrew Ross, *No-Collar: The Humane Workplace and Its Hidden Costs*, Philadelphia, Temple University Press, 2004, pp. 123-160.
[8] Andrew Ross, *The New Geography of Work: Power to the Precarious?*, in *Theory, Culture & Society* 25, no. 7-8, December 2008, p. 34.
[9] Ross, *No-Collar*, pp. 129-139.
[10] Francis Bacon, *New Atlantis* (1626), in Francis Bacon, *The Major Works*, ed. Brian Vickers, Oxford, Oxford University Press, 2002, pp. 457-490; also accessible at http://oregonstate.edu/instruct/phl302/texts/bacon/atlantis.html.

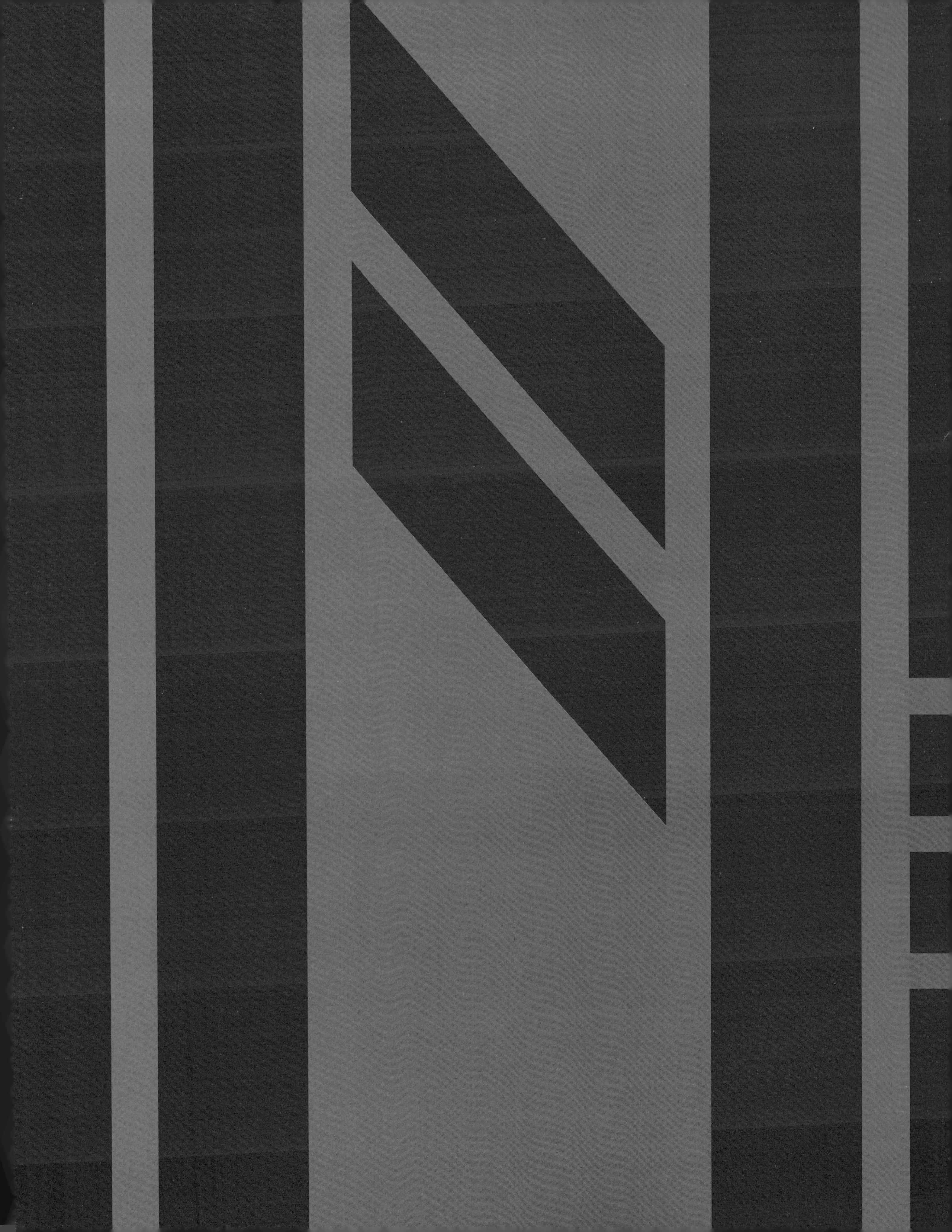

The Exhibition

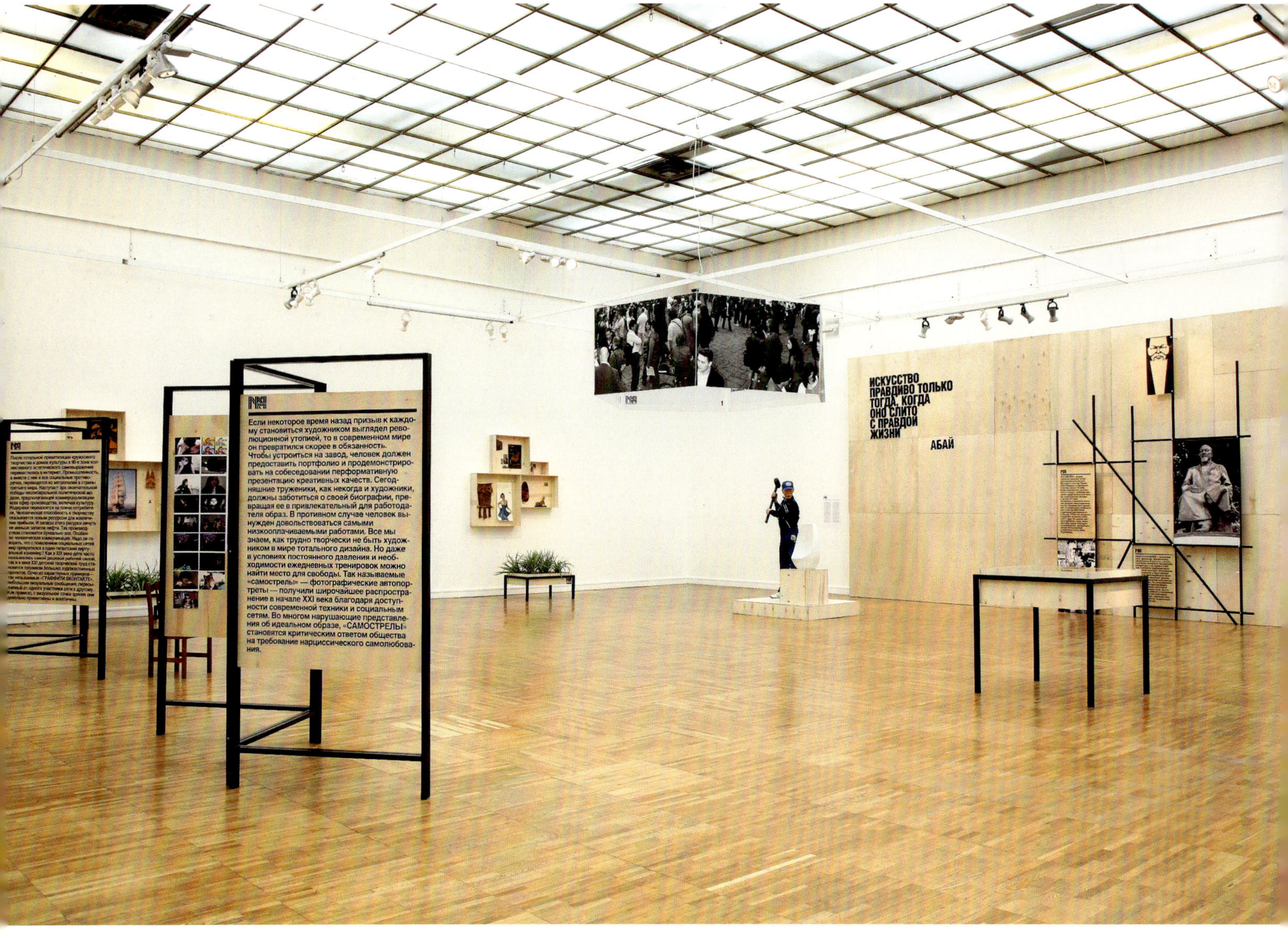
Если некоторое время назад призыв к каждому становиться художником выглядел революционной утопией, то в современном мире он превратился скорее в обязанность.
Чтобы устроиться на завод, человек должен предоставить портфолио и продемонстрировать на собеседовании перформативную презентацию креативных качеств. Сегодняшние труженики, как некогда и художники, должны заботиться о своей биографии, превращая ее в привлекательный для работодателя образ. В противном случае человек вынужден довольствоваться самыми низкооплачиваемыми работами. Все мы знаем, как трудно творчески не быть художником в мире тотального дизайна. Но даже в условиях постоянного давления и необходимости ежедневных тренировок можно найти место для свободы. Так называемые «самострелы» — фотографические автопортреты — получили широчайшее распространение в начале XXI века благодаря доступности современной техники и социальным сетям. Во многом нарушающие представления об идеальном образе, «САМОСТРЕЛЫ» становятся критическим ответом общества на требование нарциссического самолюбования.
ИСКУССТВО ПРАВДИВО ТОЛЬКО ТОГДА, КОГДА ОНО СЛИТО С ПРАВДОЙ ЖИЗНИ
АБАЙ

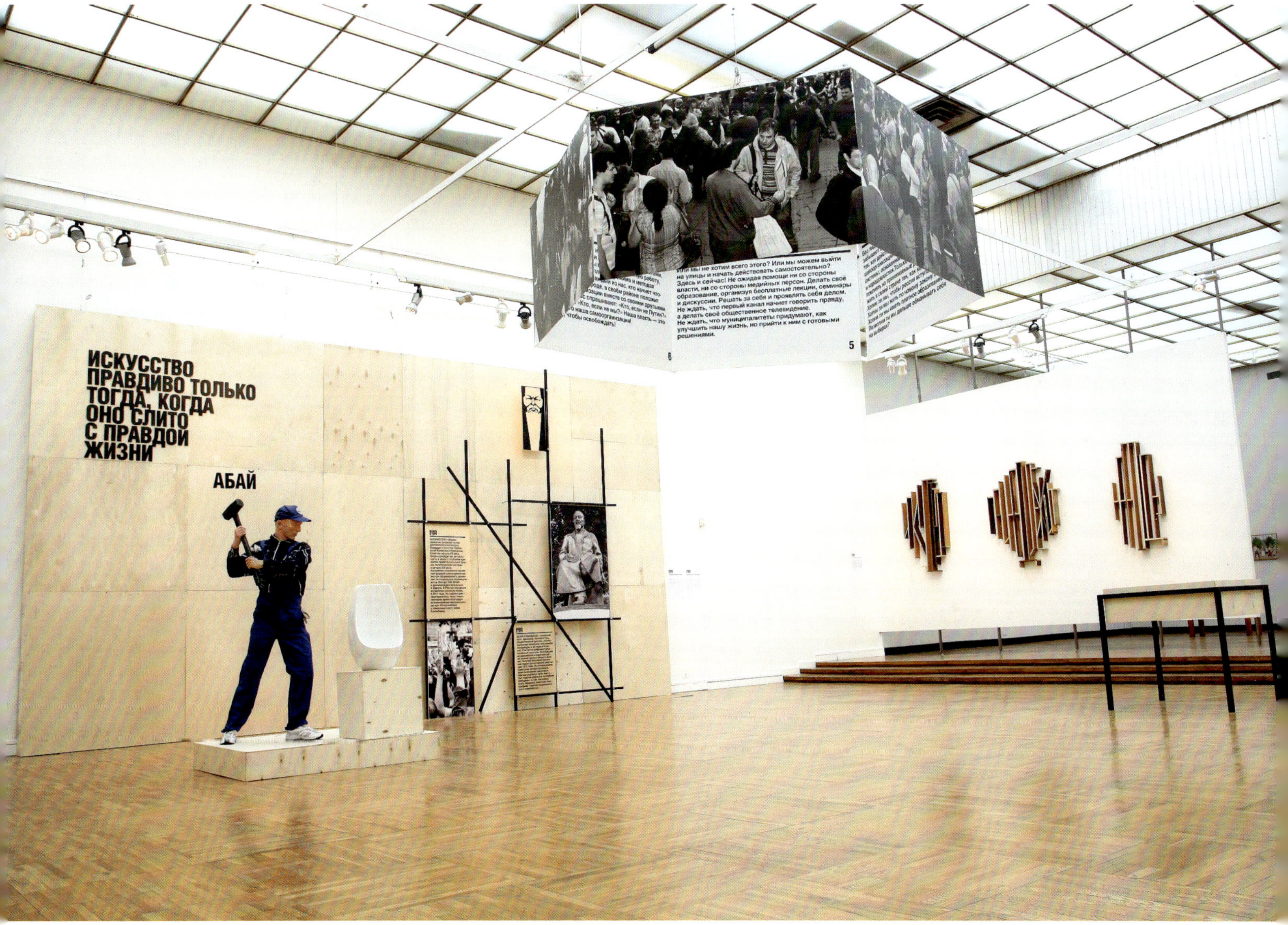
ИСКУССТВО
ПРАВДИВО ТОЛЬКО
ТОГДА, КОГДА
ОНО СЛИТО
С ПРАВДОЙ
ЖИЗНИ
АБАЙ
Или мы не хотим всего этого? Или мы можем выйти на улицы и начать действовать самостоятельно? Здесь и сейчас! Не ожидая помощи ни со стороны власти, ни со стороны медийных персон. Делать своё образование, организуя бесплатные лекции, семинары и дискуссии. Решать за себя и проявлять себя делом. Не ждать, что первый канал начнет говорить правду, а делать своё общественное телевидение. Не ждать, что муниципалитеты придумают, как улучшить нашу жизнь, но прийти к ним с готовыми решениями.
5

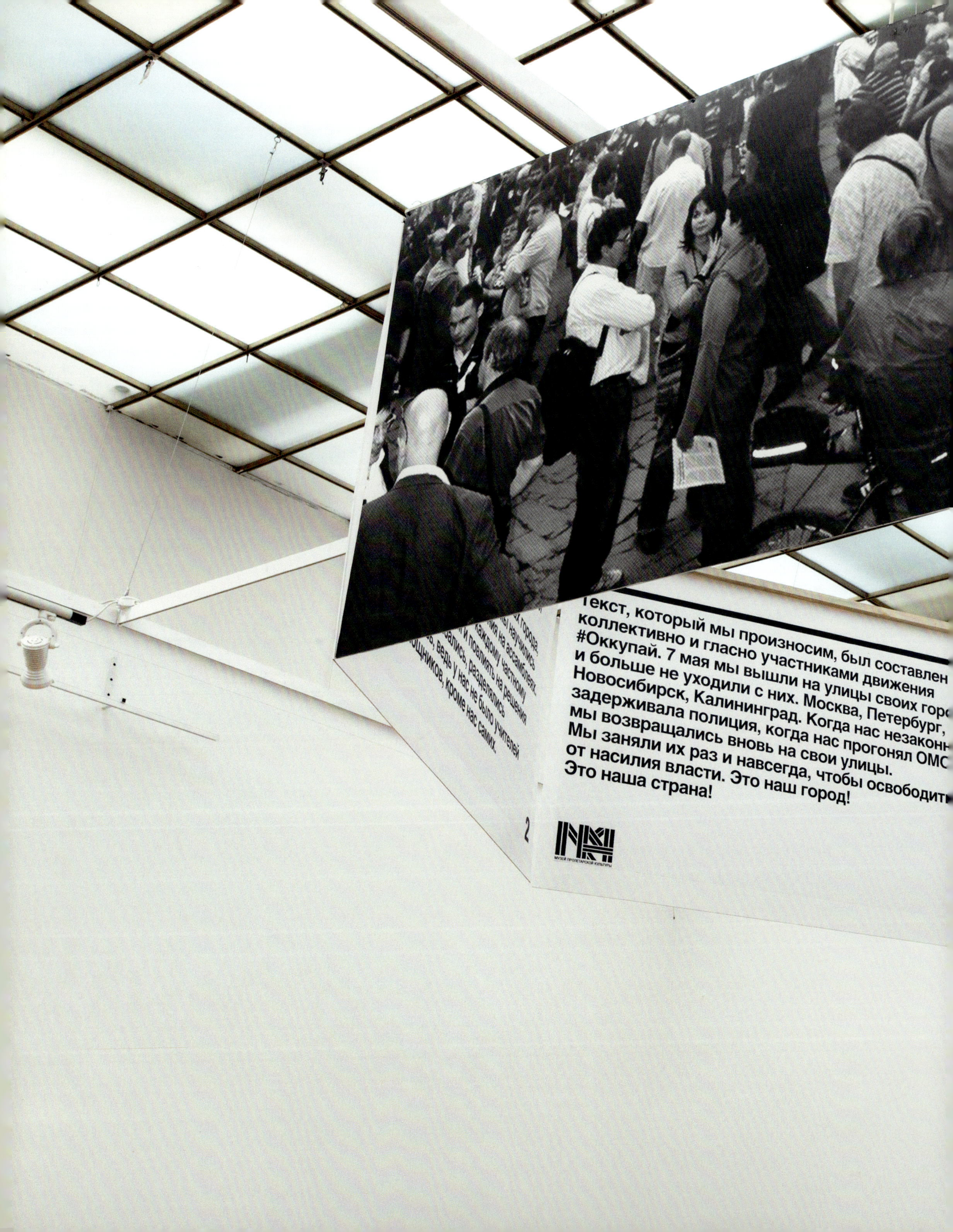
Текст, который мы произносим, был составлен
коллективно и гласно участниками движения
#Оккупай. 7 мая мы вышли на улицы своих
и больше не уходили с них. Москва, Петербург,
Новосибирск, Калининград. Когда нас
задерживала полиция, когда нас прогонял
мы возвращались вновь на свои улицы.
Мы заняли их раз и навсегда, чтобы
от насилия власти. Это наш город!
Это наша страна!

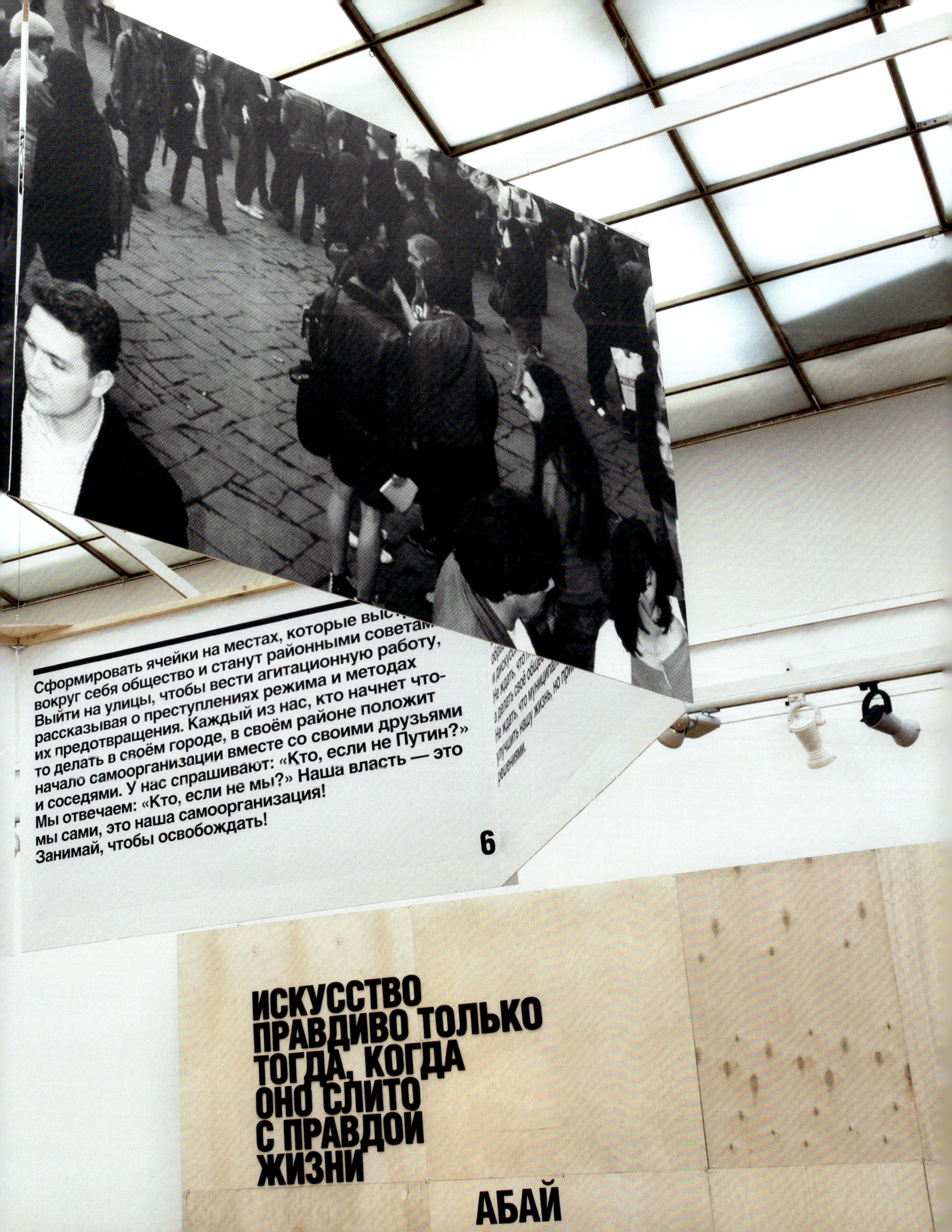
Сформировать ячейки на местах, которые выс
вокруг себя общество и станут районными совета
Выйти на улицы, чтобы вести агитационную работу,
рассказывая о преступлениях режима и методах
их предотвращения. Каждый из нас, кто начнет что-
то делать в своём городе, в своём районе положит
начало самоорганизации вместе со своими друзьями
и соседями. У нас спрашивают: «Кто, если не Путин?»
Мы отвечаем: «Кто, если не мы?» Наша власть — это
мы сами, это наша самоорганизация!
Занимай, чтобы освобождать!
6
ИСКУССТВО ПРАВДИВО ТОЛЬКО ТОГДА, КОГДА ОНО СЛИТО С ПРАВДОЙ ЖИЗНИ
АБАЙ

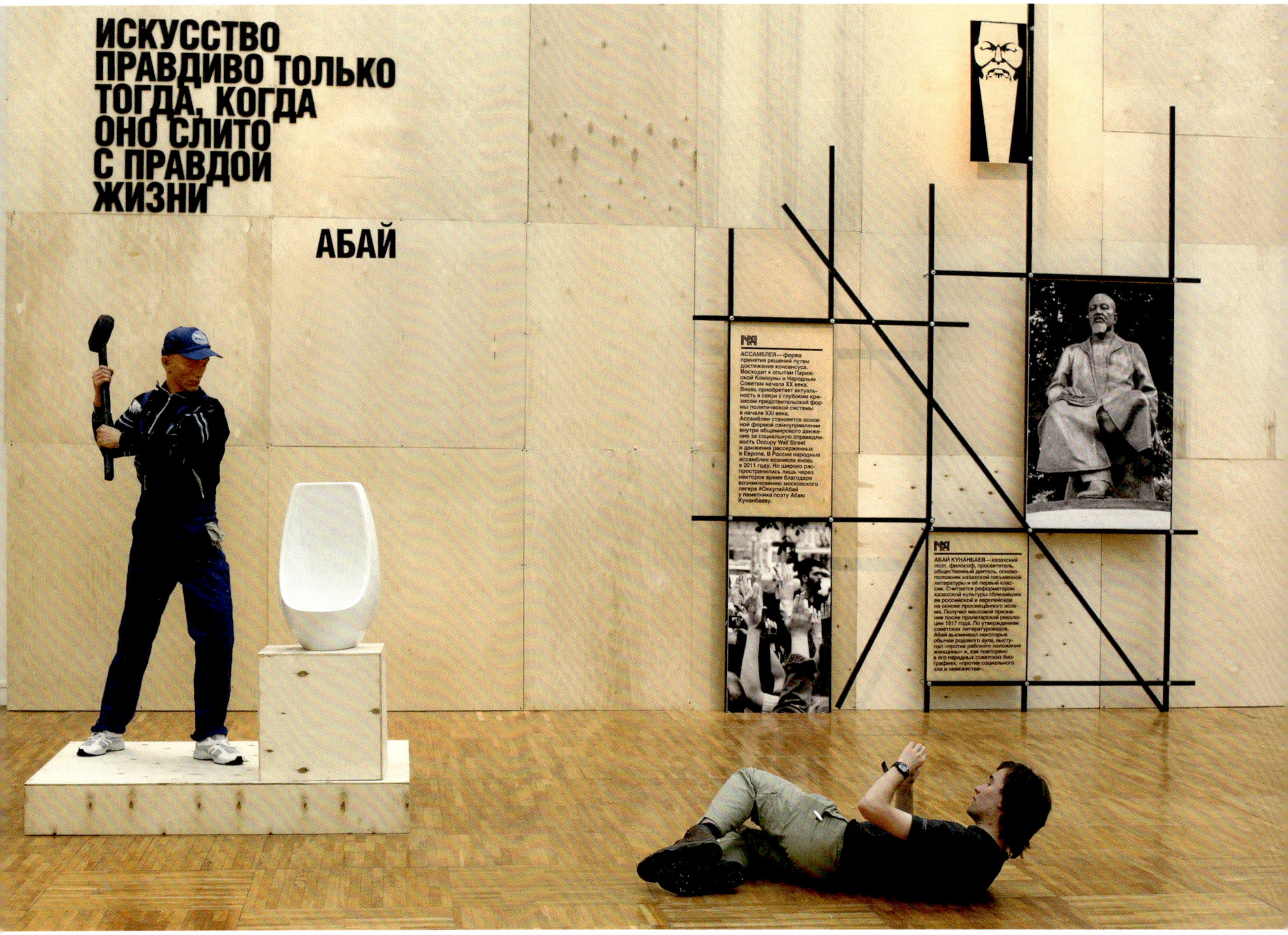
ИСКУССТВО
ПРАВДИВО ТОЛЬКО
ТОГДА, КОГДА
ОНО СЛИТО
С ПРАВДОЙ
ЖИЗНИ
АБАЙ
АССАМБЛЕЯ — форма принятия решений путем достижения консенсуса.
АБАЙ КУНАНБАЕВ — казахский поэт, философ, просветитель

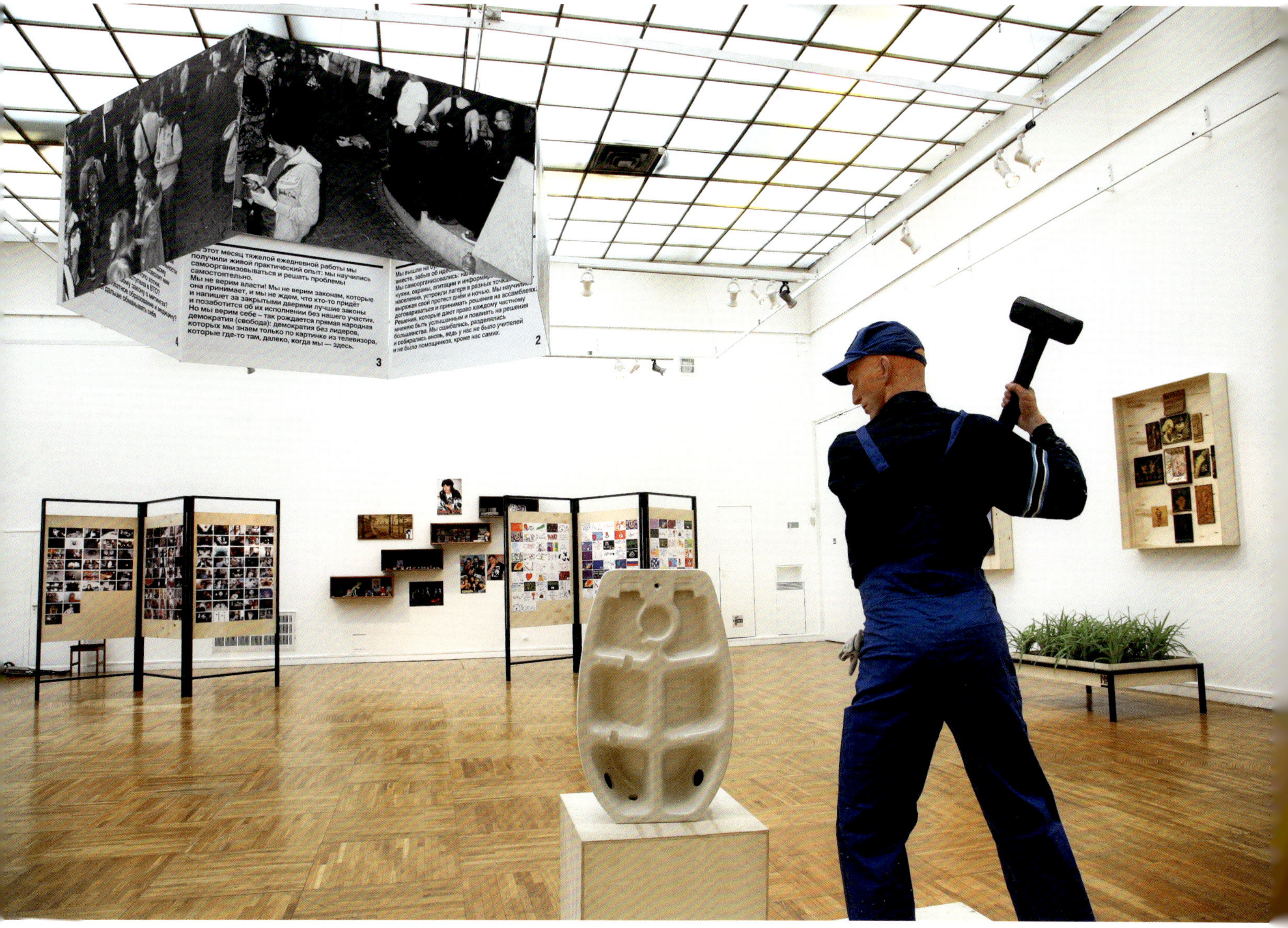
этот месяц тяжелой ежедневной работы мы
получили живой практический опыт: мы научились
самоорганизовываться и решать проблемы
самостоятельно.
Мы не верим власти! Мы не верим законам, которые
она принимает, и мы не ждем, что кто-то придёт
и напишет за закрытыми дверями лучшие законы
и позаботится об их исполнении без нашего участия.
Но мы верим себе – так рождается прямая народная
демократия (свобода): демократия без лидеров,
которых мы знаем только по картинке из телевизора,
которые где-то там, далеко, когда мы — здесь.
3
выражая свой протест днём и ночью. Мы научились
договариваться и принимать решения на ассамблеях.
Решения, которые дают право каждому частному
мнению быть услышанным и повлиять на решения
большинства. Мы ошибались, разделялись
и собирались вновь, ведь у нас не было учителей
и не было помощников, кроме нас самих.
2

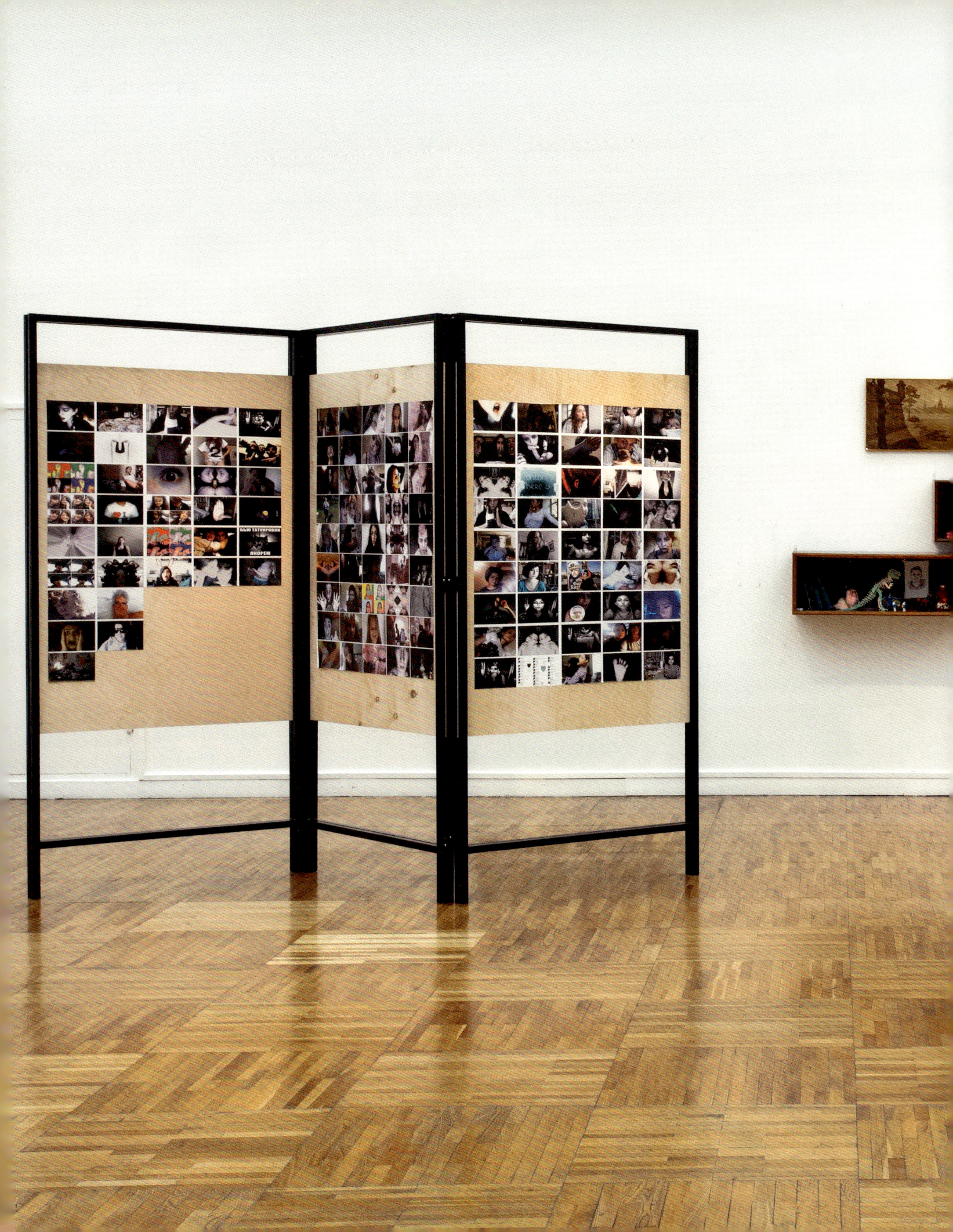
БЬЮ ТАТУИРОВКИ
ЯКОРЕМ

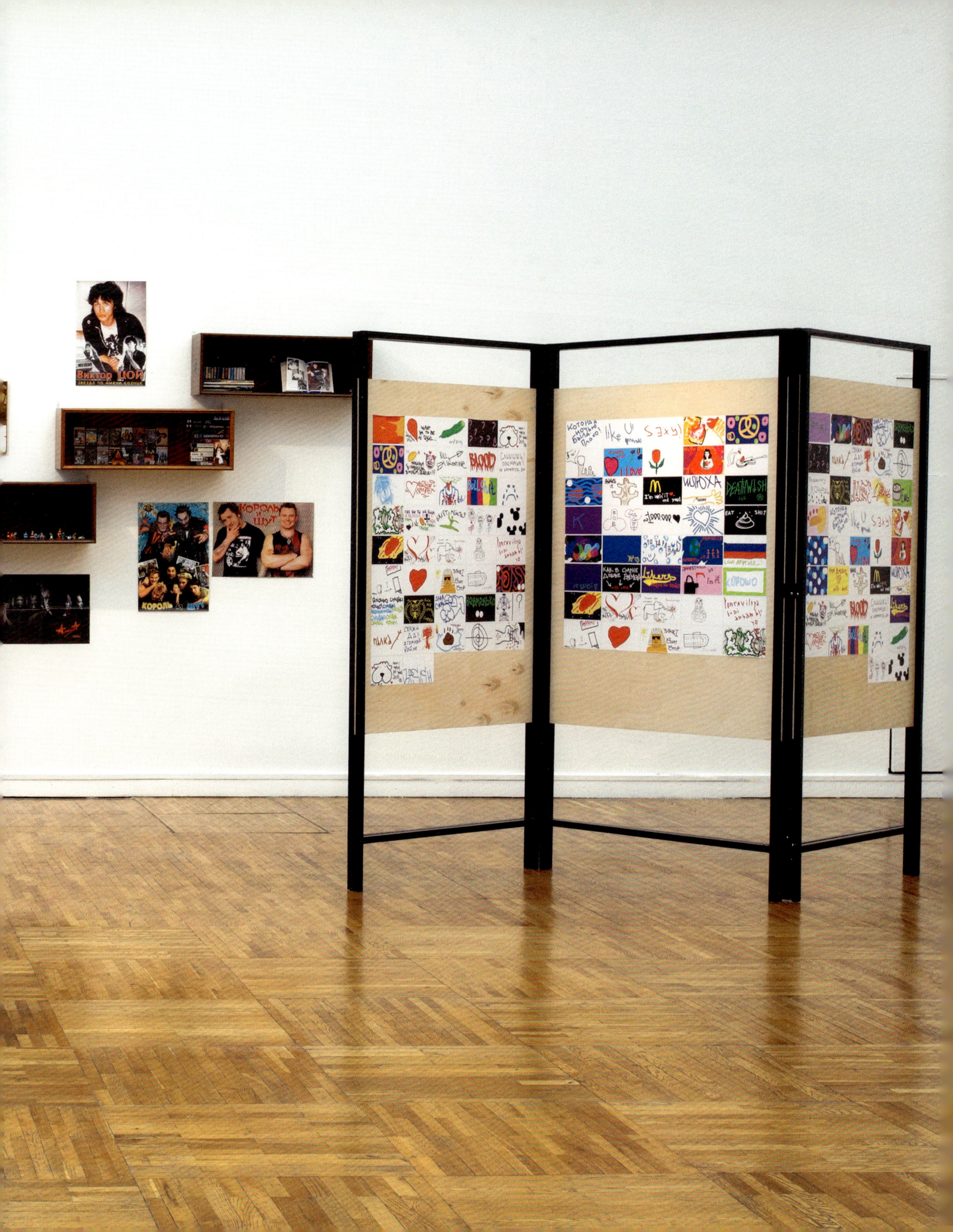
Виктор ЦОЙ
BLOOD
DEATHWISH
like U
EAT SHIT

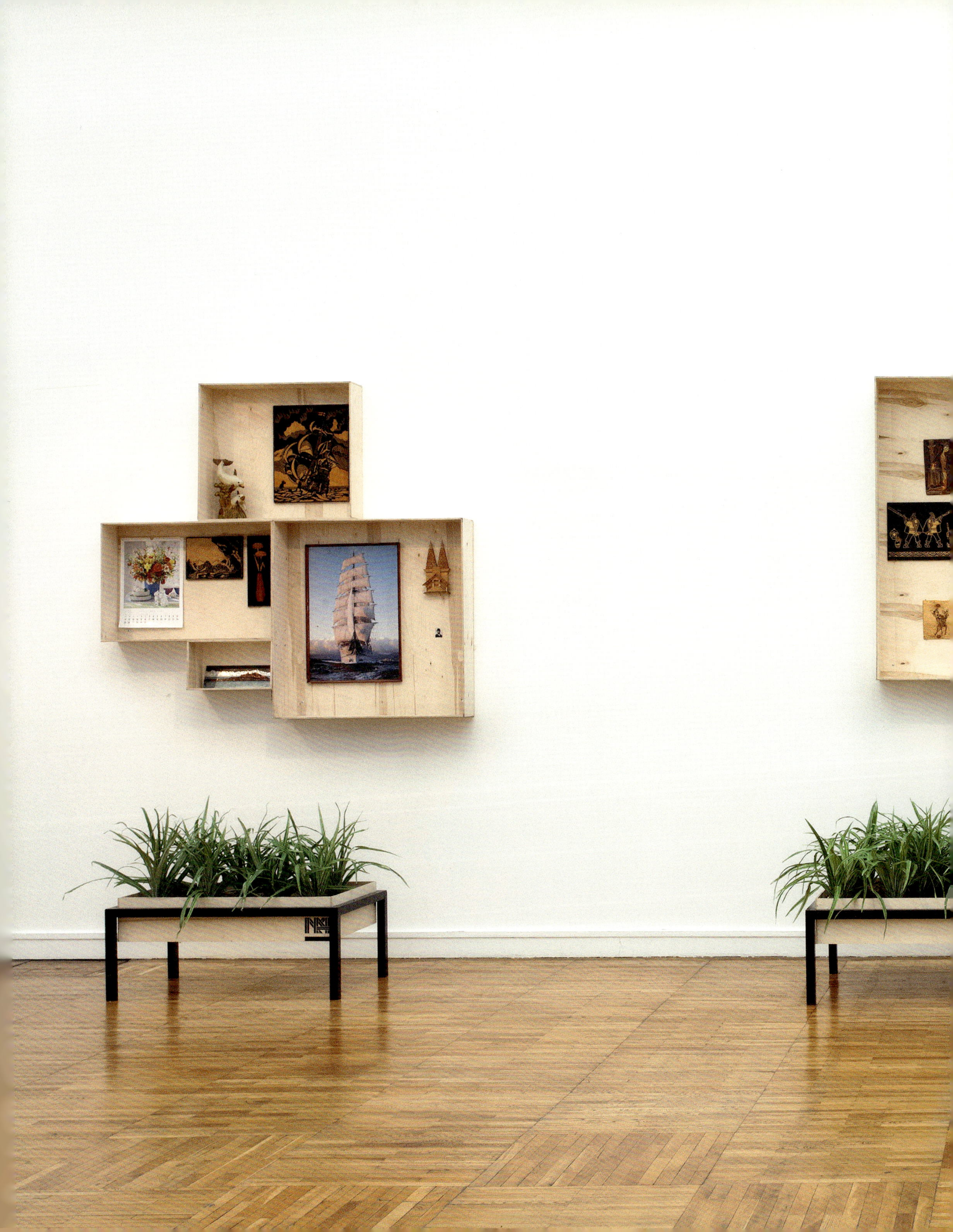

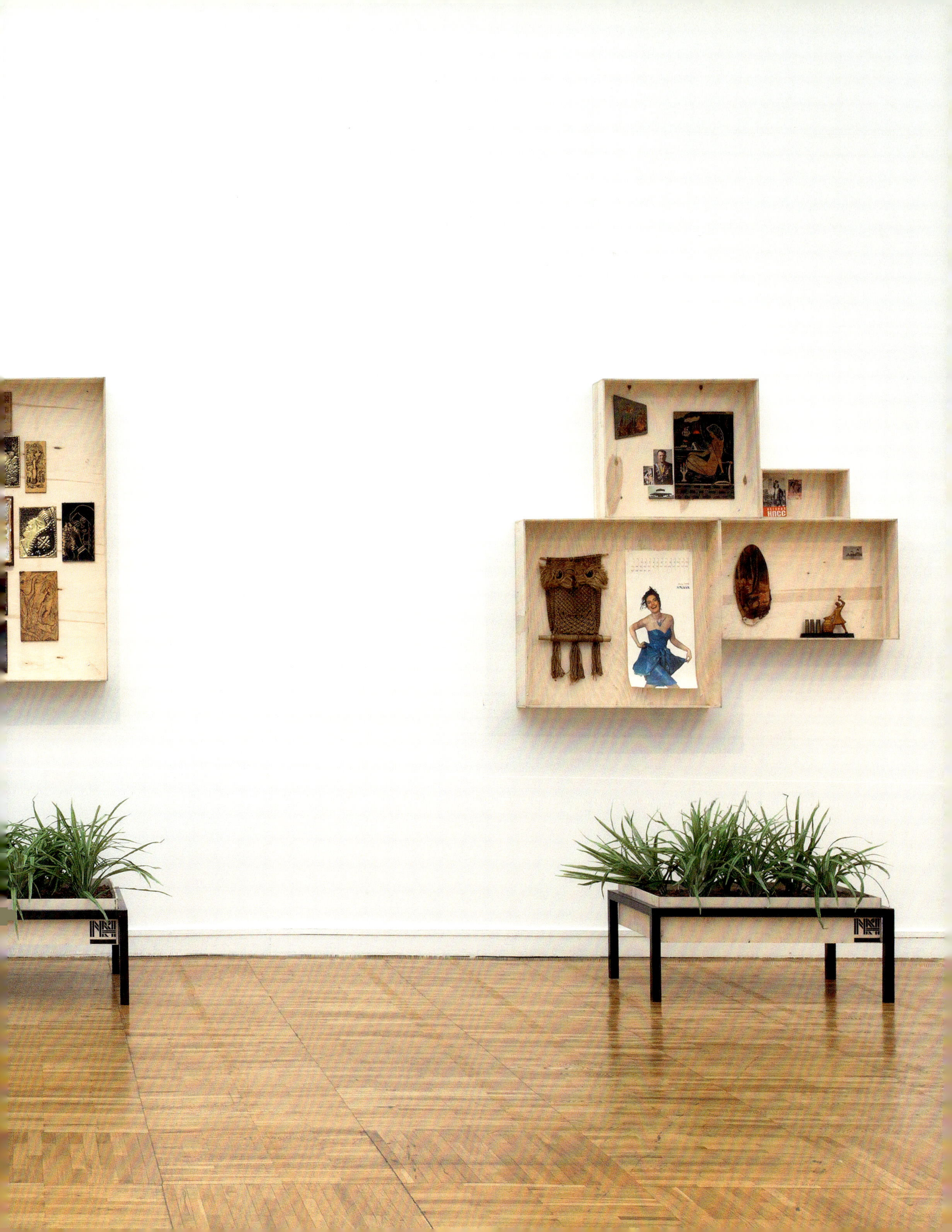

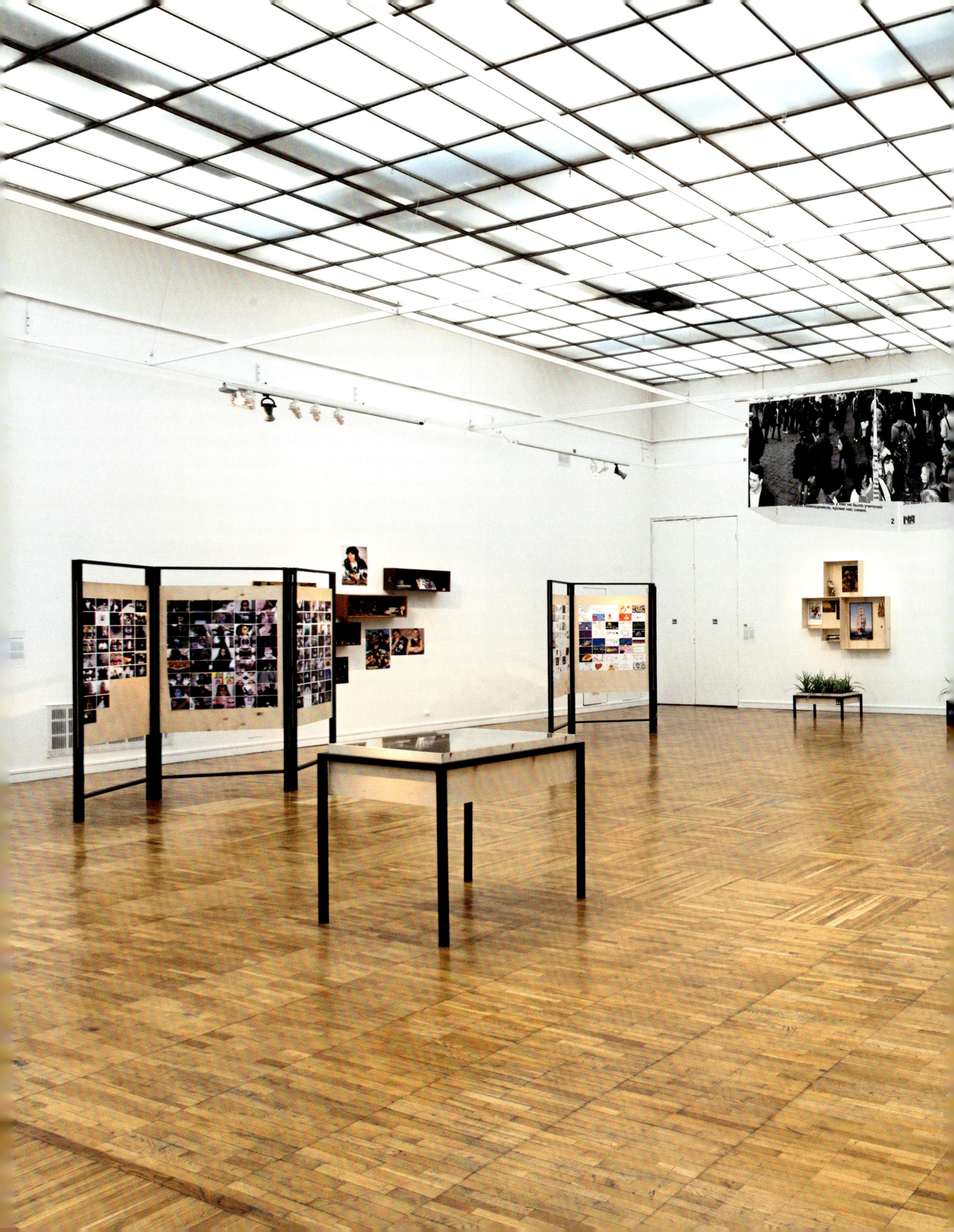
у нас не было учителей
помощников, кроме нас самих.
2

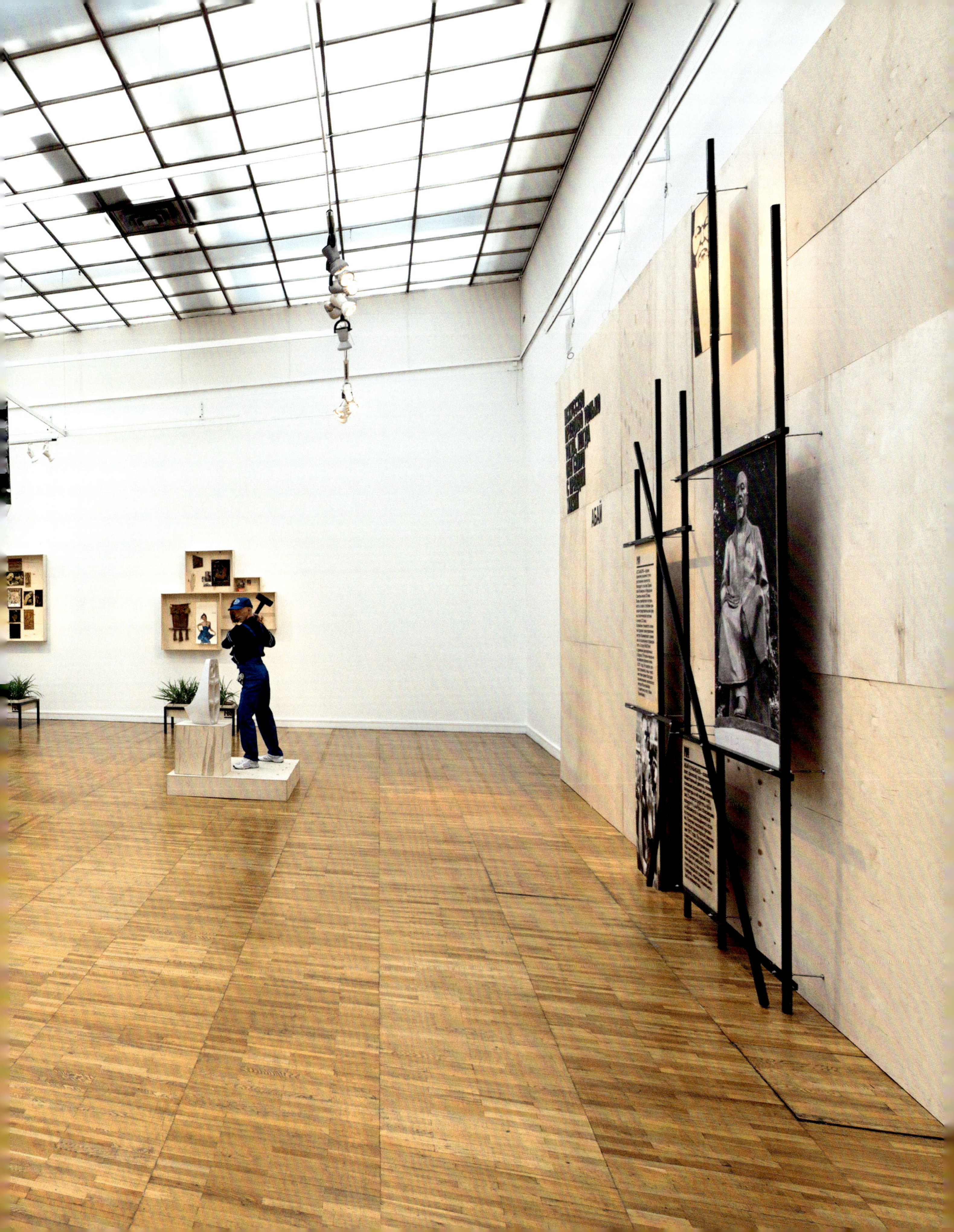
АБАЙ

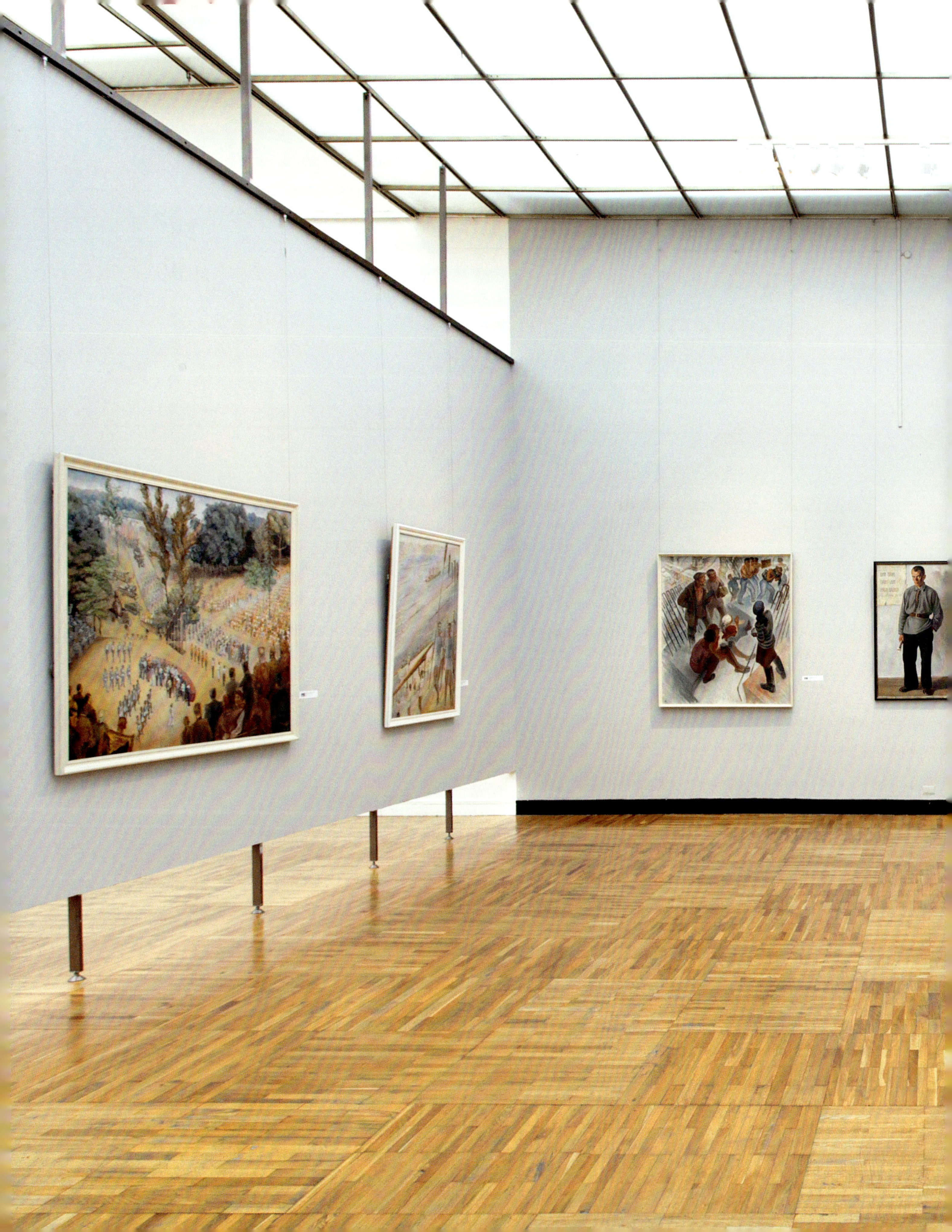

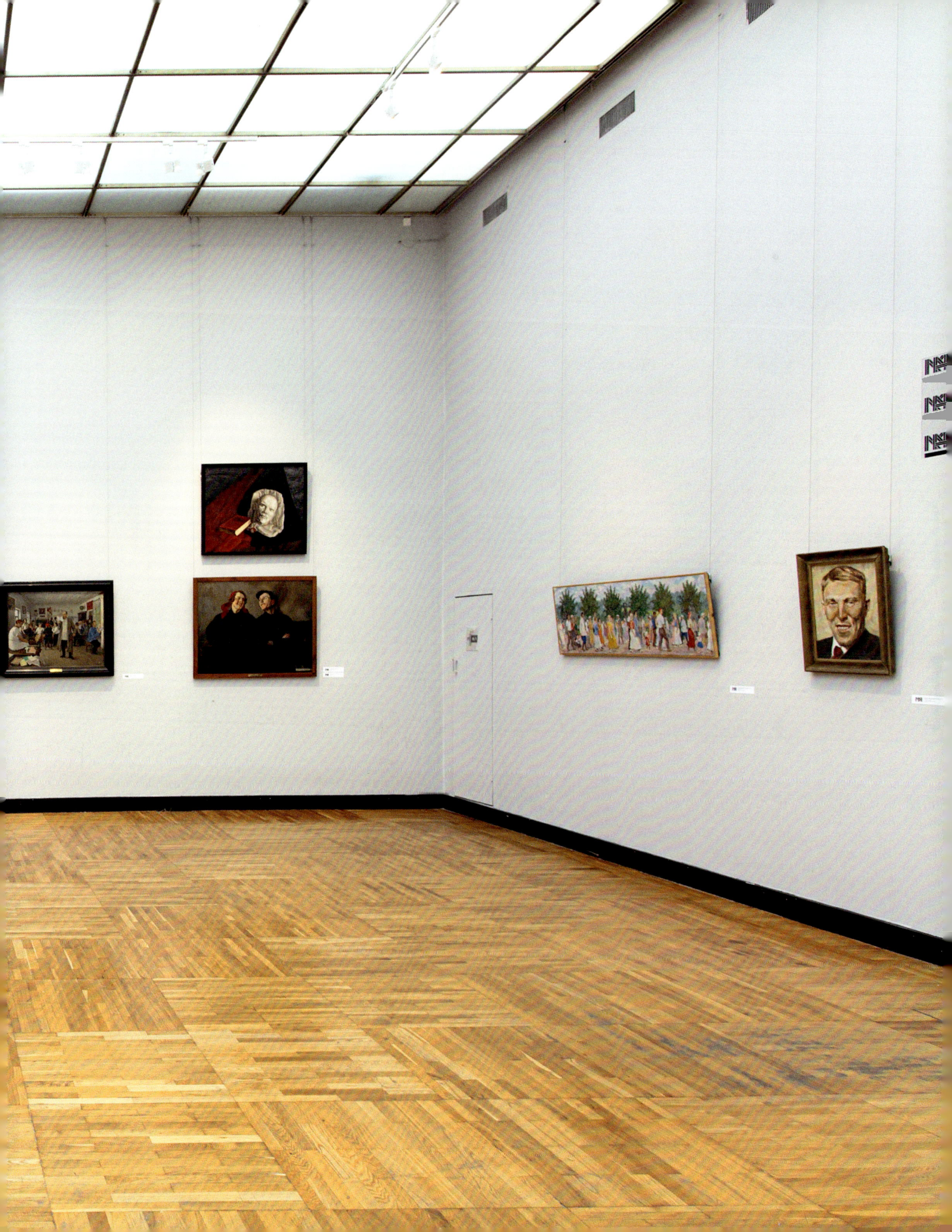

Art Belongs to the People

Ruben Beloglazov was known primarily as a great professional, a master of his craft, and simply as a decent person. The Soviet engineer did not have an easy life. He was born in Voronezh shortly before the war. His childhood took place during the grim years of deprivation. Beloglazov lost his parents at a young age, and was raised in the large family of his aunt. Even as a boy, he showed an interest in inventing things; this interest later grew to encompass the hard sciences and affected his choice of profession. He was a straight-A student and Communist Party member, but also a joker and the life of the party. He could spend hours reading Mayakovsky. Friends and acquaintances described Ruben Beloglazov as a sensitive man who was ready to help at any time. Everyone knew his culinary talents. An exemplary family man, Beloglazov loved noisy gatherings. He liked to invite his friends to his dacha on the weekends and show them the furnishings he had created. This is how family and friends remember him. However, it was only years later that Ruben Beloglazov's artistic legacy was appreciated. Today, he is considered a classic designer. Amidst complex political and economic conditions, Beloglazov and thousands of similar ordinary Soviet workers and engineers managed to maintain popular art at the highest level. Beloglazov's capacious and concise interior designs were always based the new communist way of life's inextricable link with the proletariat's emancipatory mission and the leading role of the Party. The Voronezh Local History Museum contains several wall-mounted shelves in the shape of slogans rendered in constructivist fonts. *Art Belongs to the People* is a reconstruction of one of Beloglazov's unpreserved works from the late 1960s.

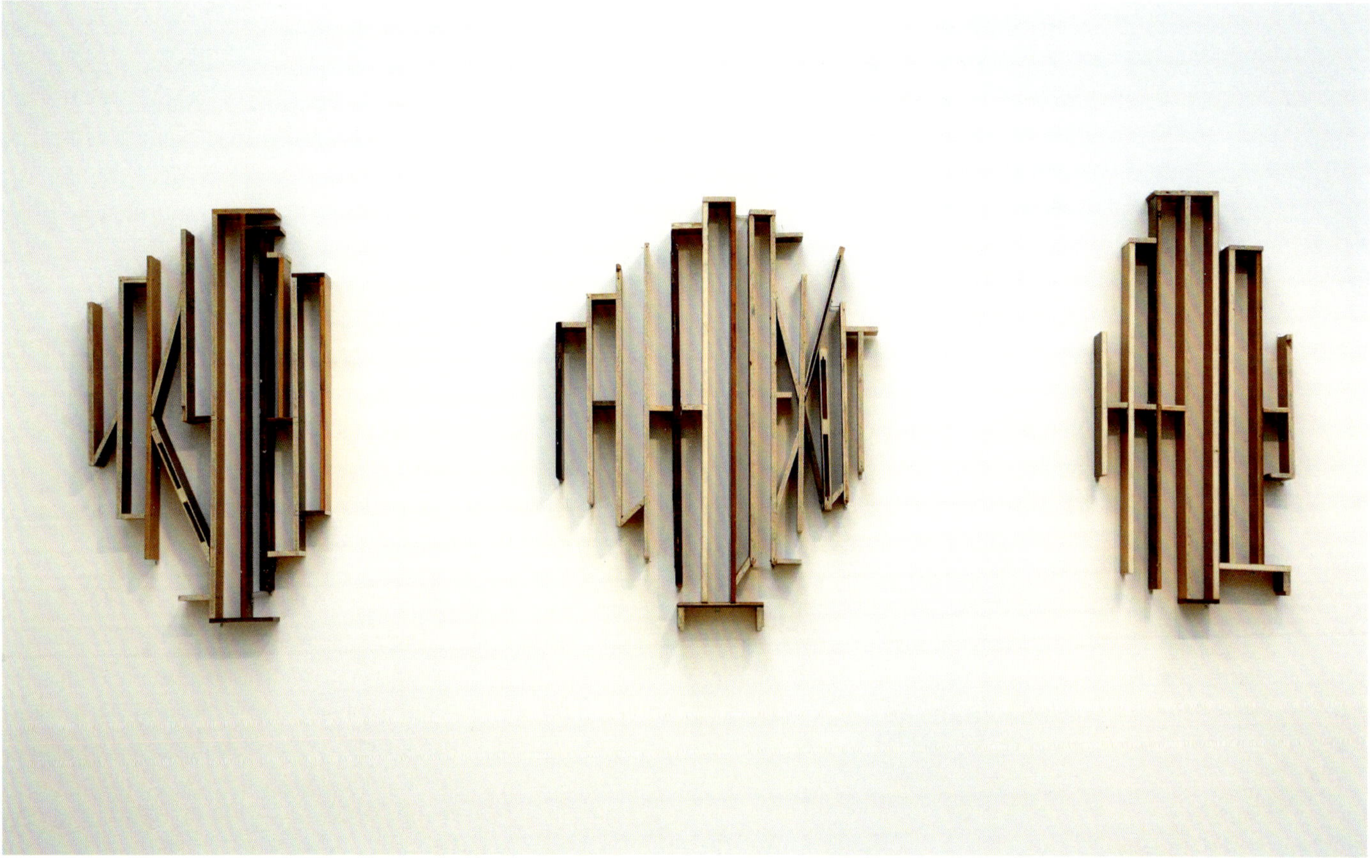

Model No. 14

Ilya Dondurenko spent his entire adult life working on the railroad in the village of Sokoliki. Researchers have noted that even in childhood the future folk artist showed remarkable learning abilities. Straight-A student Dondurenko was always an example to his peers. After graduating from high school with honors and dreaming of travel, he enrolled at Voronezh Railway Technical School. This bizarre decision was dictated by the notion that only what was "common" would be relevant in the future. There was no point in entertaining hopes of personal success or being satisfied by hobbies. All people on the earth needed to travel, and that meant it was necessary to create the conditions for this by building railways and railway stations, and engineering new types of trains, airplanes, ships, and space ships. A devoted Marxist from an early age, Dondurenko decided he should devote himself to physical, truly proletarian labor. Thanks to Dondurenko, thousands of miles of railway track were laid in our country. Our cities become closer to each other, and the people who lived in them became more intellectually and spiritually well rounded. Until the end of his life, Dondurenko fashioned architectural models from matches. Our collection includes one of his earliest models, *Model No. 14*. It demonstrates a highly developed artistic imagination and a profound understanding of the proletariat's role in humanity's destiny. The model depicts a constructivist building in the shape of a hammer and sickle, which has been turned into a church of the people. Realizing the conventional appeal of religious themes, Dondurenko, who grew up in a rural peasant community, preserved this motif as an essential metaphor. Indeed, from ancient times until the first socialist revolutions, people searched in the divine realm for solutions to economic and political problems.

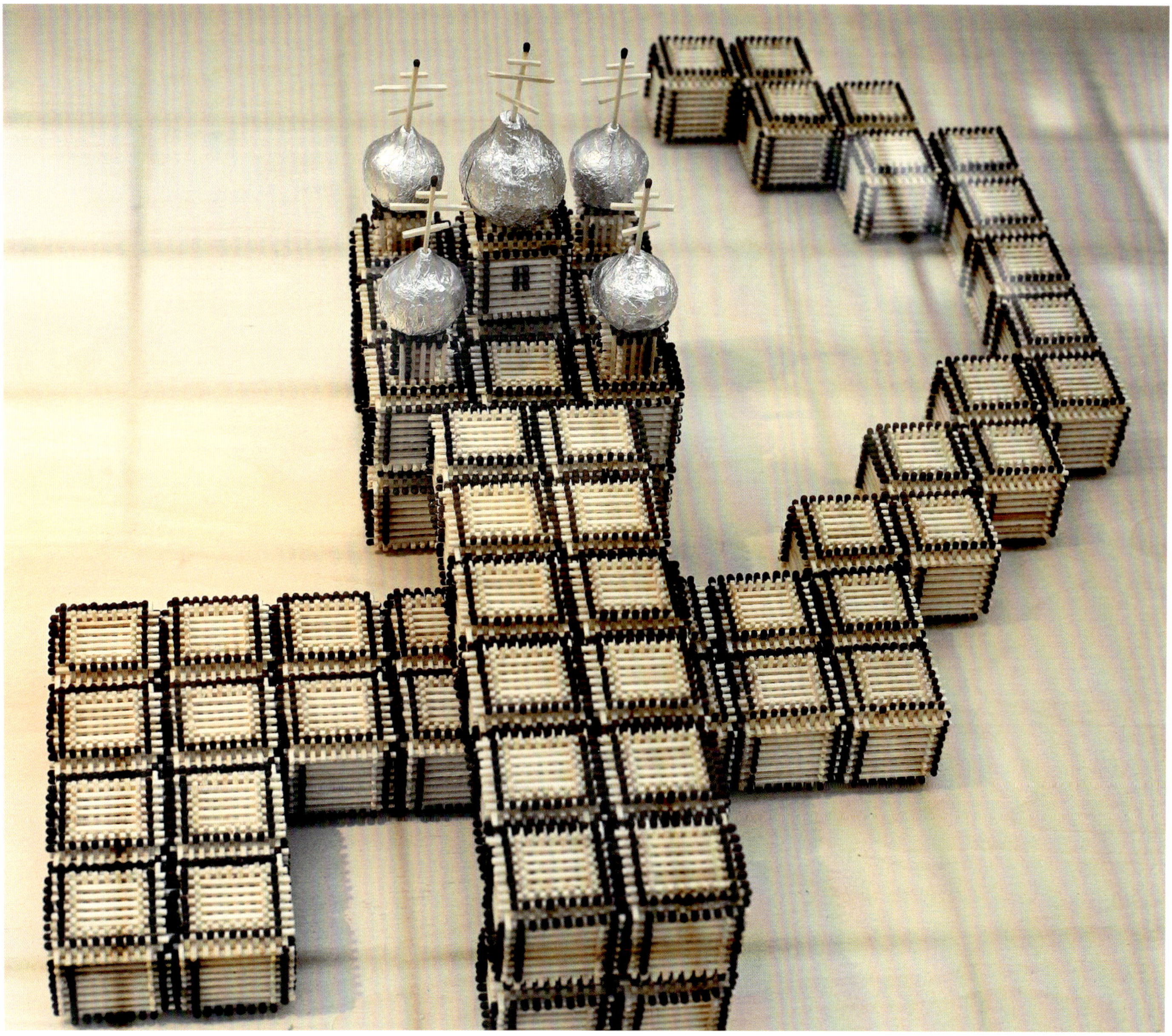

Collages 1980s

Collage remains one of the most common varieties of proletarian art. Modernist artists developed collage technique in the early twentieth century, but it became widespread amongst workers only in the 1970s and 1980s. At any rate, the most "ancient" of the found specimens date to this period. One of the main reasons for the spread of individual collages and even entire giant altars in production facilities is the development of the printing industry, whose products gradually became better and more affordable. Workers used accessible and widespread images from popular culture to create their collages. The most popular were images of singers, popular actors, politicians and sports figures, landmarks, and, more rarely, nature scenes. Images of a sexual nature, graphic design for food products, and religiously symbolic images are generally categorized separately. The creation of anonymous collages harks back to the practice of decorating dwellings and the folk art of the pre-industrial era. Typically, such decorations were imbued with religious meaning and had not only an aesthetic function but also a ritual and sometimes even magical function.

The brutal visuality of industrial collages expresses the contradictions in the lives of industrial workers in the twentieth century. On the one hand, many workers in developed capitalist countries, especially after the events of the late 1960s, were able to enjoy mass consumption, which reduced the level of their discontent and made them less revolutionary. On the other hand, the tactical concessions made by capitalists, who thus "fattened" workers, were still unable to resolve class antagonisms. The aspirations of producers, which were not satisfied by the frenzy of consumer society, took on a new – creative – aspect. In the Soviet Union and later, during the post-Soviet period, consumer society's level of development was quite different, as reflected in the specific materials used in collages. In the artworks of the time, we can see an attempt to escape from the routines of production, which stalled due to inefficient bureaucratic management. It is difficult to imagine, but alienating mechanical labor was not so long ago considered natural, even in countries that were formally socialist.

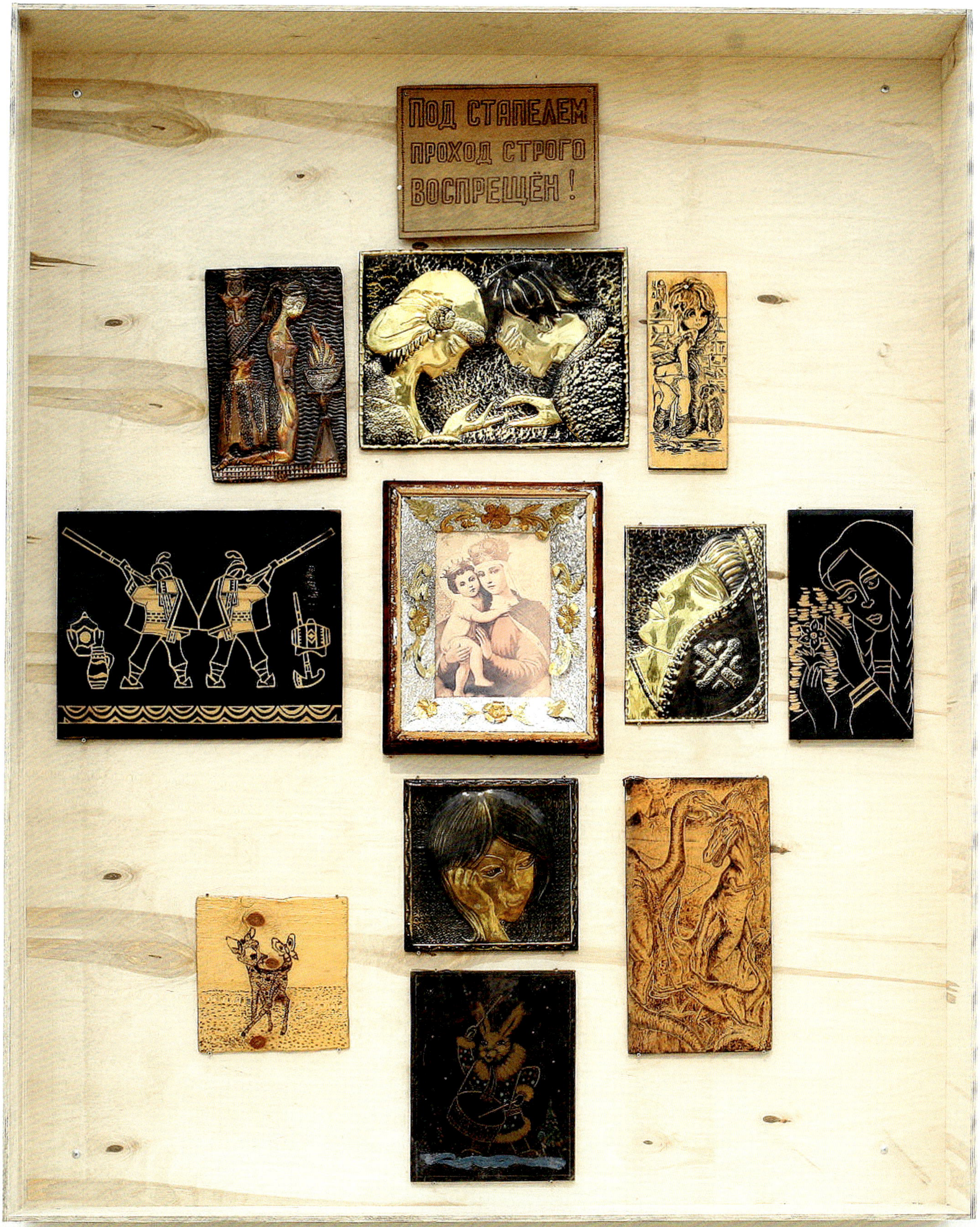
Под стапелем
проход строго
воспрещён !

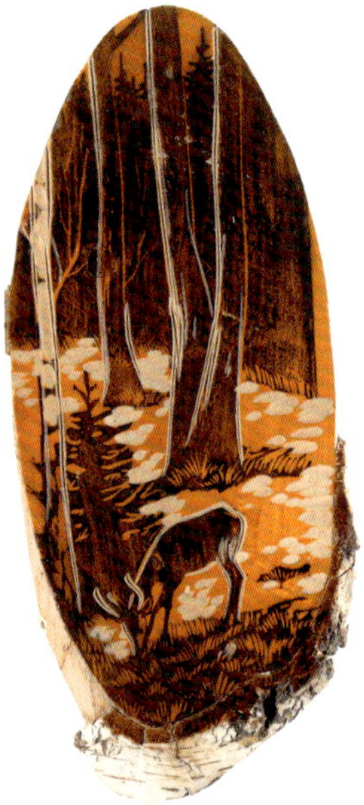

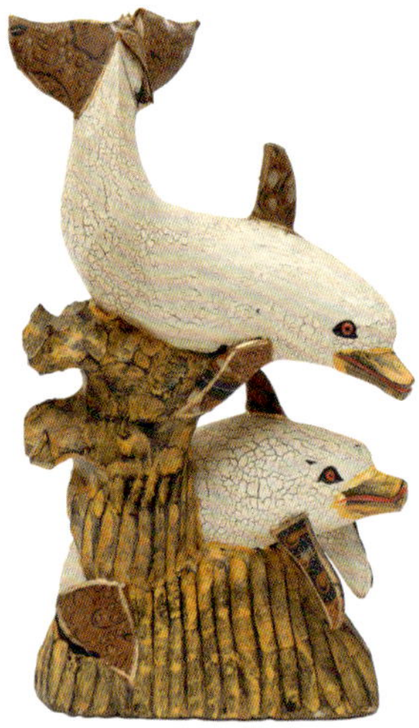

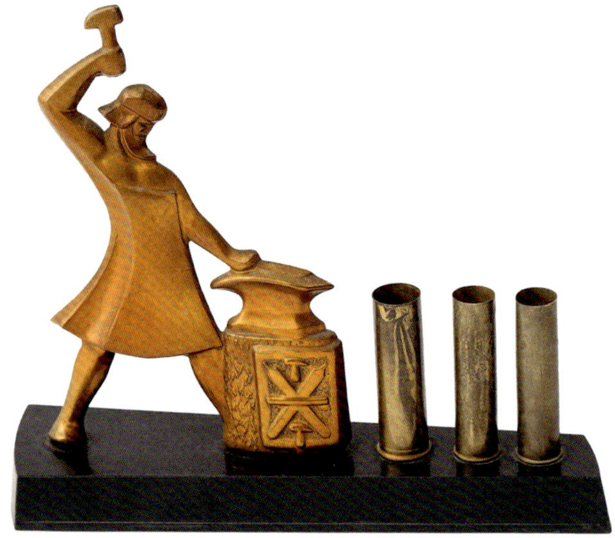

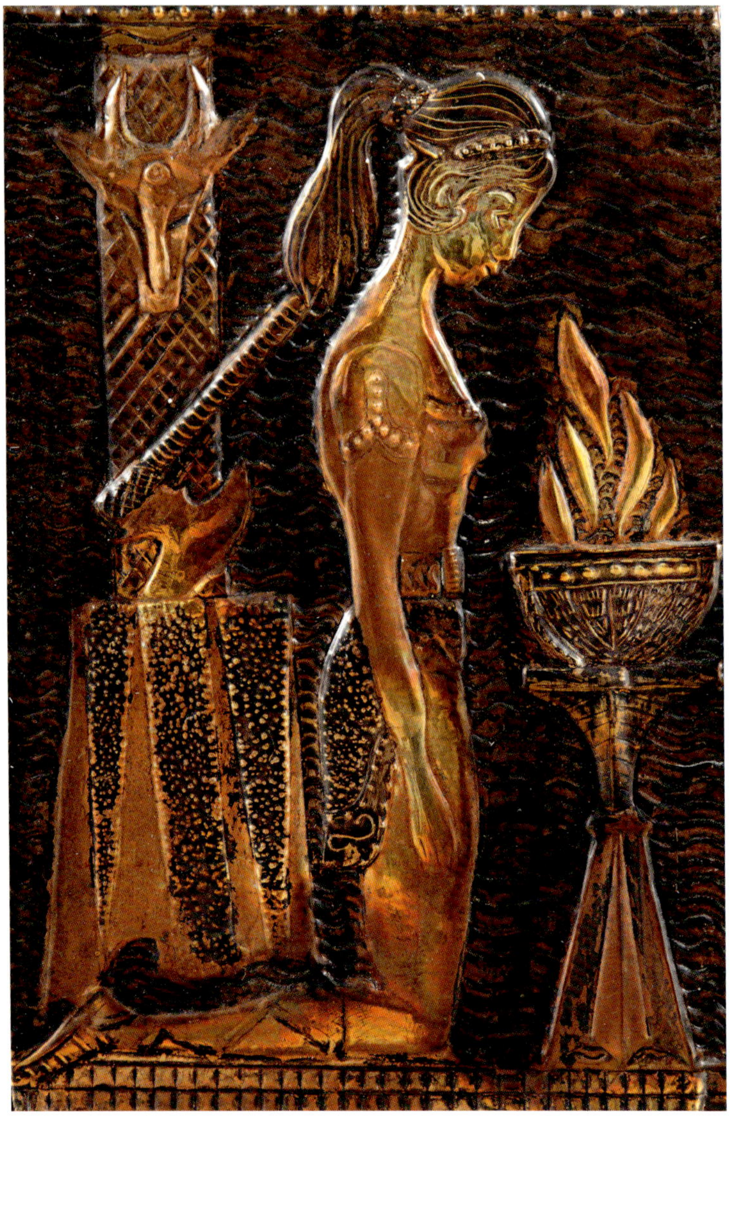

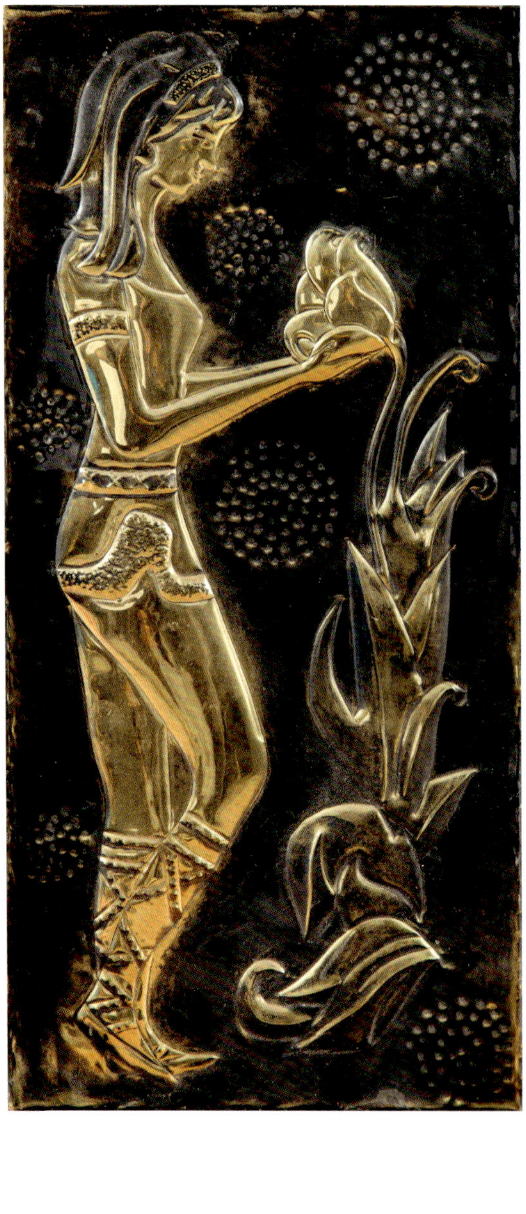

recognition of individual freedom and human dignity.

6. Consensus. Our method is to find solutions that take into account all personal opinions and are based on the mutual consent of participants.

Manifesto of the Occupy Movement in Russia

The text we are going to read aloud was composed collectively and publicly by members of the Occupy movement.

On May 7 we took to the streets of our cities and remained there. Moscow, Petersburg, Novosibirsk, Kaliningrad. When we were illegally detained by the police, when the riot cops chased us away, we returned again to our streets, we occupied them once and for all in order to liberate them from the violence of the authorities. This is our city! This is our country!

We took to the boulevards and squares, and began living together, setting aside ideologies and disagreements. We organized ourselves. We got field kitchens, security and public awareness campaigns up and running. We set up camps at various points in the city to protest day and night.

We learned to negotiate with one another and make decisions at General Assemblies, decisions that give every individual opinion the right to be heard and to influence the decision of the majority. We made mistakes, suffered divisions and came together again, for we had no teachers and no one to help us except ourselves.

Over this month of hard daily work we have gained practical experience: we have learned to organize ourselves and solve problems independently.

We do not trust the authorities. We do no trust the laws they pass, and we do not expect someone to come along and write better laws behind closed doors and make sure they are enforced without our involvement.

But we trust ourselves: this is how direct popular democracy is born. A democracy without leaders whom we only know from TV screens, leaders who are somewhere far away, while we are right here. A democracy without leaders who forget about us as soon as they have clawed their way to the top.

You cannot change the system by acting the way the system does. The goal of our self-organization is to build a different political system, a system based on the principles of horizontality and democracy.

Only the opportunity for each person to influence how decisions are made will enable us to live in our country the way we want to live.

Do we want Russia to join the WTO?

Do we want to live under the new law on demonstrations?

Do we want to have commercialized education and medical care?

Will we continue to let ourselves be duped during elections?

Or do we not want all this?

Or can we take to the streets and begin acting independently? Right here, right now, without waiting for help from the authorities or media personalities?

We can make our own education by organizing free lectures, seminars and discussions. Make our own decisions and prove ourselves by getting things done. Make our own public television rather than waiting for Channel One to tell the truth. Come to municipal governments with ready-made solutions rather than waiting for them to figure out how to improve our lives. Form cells on the ground that will organize society around them and become district councils. Take to the streets with public awareness campaigns, telling people about the crimes of the regime and how to stop them.

Each of us who begins doing something in their cities, in their districts, lays the foundations of self-organization along with their friends and neighbors.

We are asked, "If not Putin, then who?"

We reply, "Who if not us?"

We ourselves, our self-organization, are the powers that be! Occupy in order to liberate!

Revolutionary Museum and Museum of Revolution

Principles of Art Museum Development

Alexei Fedorov-Davydov

The tradition of all dead
generations weighs like
a nightmare on the minds
of the living.
Karl Marx, *The Eighteenth Brumaire of Louis Bonaparte*

1. Our achievements in the field of museum development are well known and acknowledged. I do not want to downplay them, much less ignore them. But, amidst the fast pace of our progress, yesterday's achievements no longer satisfy us today. We are restless and insatiable in our demands, in setting ourselves more and more new objectives. This is the token and guarantee of our growth's organicness and revolutionary nature.

2. Examining museum development and its achievements over the past eleven revolutionary years within the overall context of culture building, one is surprised not at how much has been done, but rather at how little has been done. We have to admit that the revolution still has not taken place in terms of fundamental directives for the art museum field. The ideological positions remain what they were, that is, bourgeois and idealistic. The achievements themselves and the growth have been the achievements, growth, and self-affirmation of these bourgeois-idealist positions.

3. This should not surprise Marxists. It should be borne in mind that the proletarian revolution, while pursuing its own specific objectives, was to have concurrently realized and brought to completion the objectives of the bourgeois revolution. The political regime of the aristocratic-bureaucratic monarchy hindered the development not only of proletarian but also of advanced bourgeois culture and ideology. The proletarian revolution liberated this advanced bourgeois culture, which in the first phase of the revolution shared its goals to a certain extent.

4. The nationalization of major private art collections, which dealt a blow to the ideology of property, the main pillar of the bourgeois mentality, should not mislead us as to the nature of this revolutionary act's culture use. For we are dealing here with advanced, that is, radical, bourgeois artistic ideology, which to a certain extent and under certain conditions is even "revolutionary." For it, private, scattered, and chaotic art collections were already a past stage of museum construction.

5. In the mass, museum workers were, in terms of their class nature, members of the radical petit bourgeois intelligentsia, which did not have large amounts of capital and did not suffer from requisitions. For this intelligentsia, collecting valuable artworks and antiques from country and urban "nests of the gentlefolk," unearthing "pearls" amidst the junk in the collections of bourgeois merchants, uncovering frescoes and icons in monasteries, freeing old buildings from later additions, and turning religious relics into museum artifacts were fully their "vocation." Indeed, requisition and collecting valuables for museums gave bourgeois artistic amateurism hitherto unprecedented opportunities. What had been hidden under vestments in churches and guarded by monks from the depredations of the godless, what had rotted and crumbled on country estates, was retrieved, uncovered, and studied.
After the revolution, museum workers and enthusiasts began realizing on a national scale, with the forces and resources of the state apparatus, what before the revolution they carried out privately and artisanally, and what had been associated with such undertakings as the publication *Old Years*, the *Historical Exhibition of Portraits* of 1905, the *Historical Exhibition of Architecture* of 1911, the *Exhibition of Icons* of 1913, the restoration of the Church of the Savior on

the Nereditsa, Ovruch Cathedral, and so on and so forth. Art museum development basically came down to collecting, preserving, and restoring old works of art.

6. The few pre-revolutionary museums, whether "imperial" (the Hermitage, the Russian Museum) or municipal (the Tretyakov State Gallery), which were managed by senior officials and dependent on sluggish, uncultured municipal governments, were disorderly warehouses, unsystematic chambers of curiosities. They were incapable of satisfying "European" standards of whatever sort. Before the revolution, reforming them was almost impossible or extremely difficult (remember the uproar over Grabarev's rehanging of the Tretyakov State Gallery). During the years of the revolution, reforming these museums has involved typifying them, supplementing and, conversely, eliminating a number of artifacts, and, finally, in carrying out a primary and chronologically primitive systematization of the collections. This reform turned them in cultural bourgeois museums on the model of the advanced museums in capitalist countries, but no more than that, as anyone can attest to who has seen, at least, the latest hangings in the Hermitage and Tretyakov State Gallery.

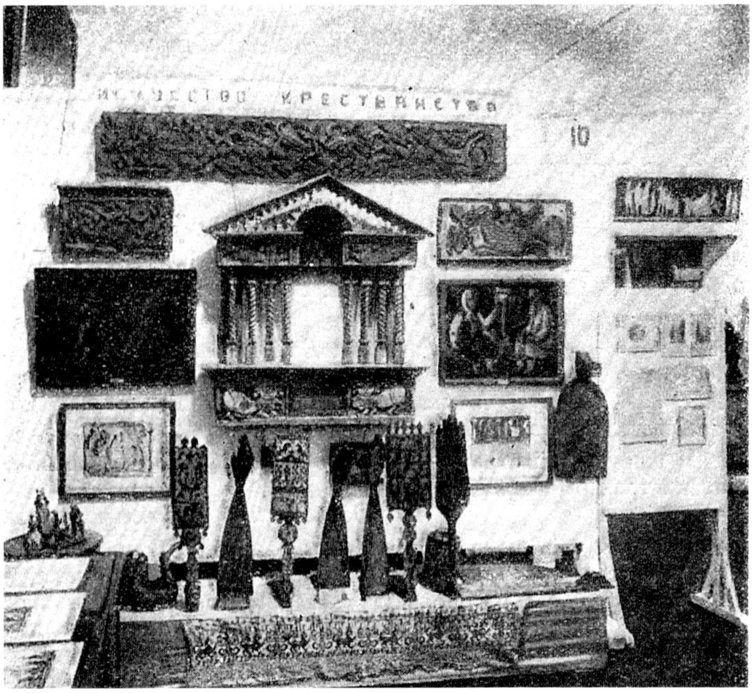

7. The same can be said about museums of so-called decorative art (the Armory, the Furniture Museum, the Porcelain Museum etc.) and estate museums. What has been done to Detskoye Selo and Gatchina, to Arkhangelskoye and Ostankino in terms of turning them into museums differs quite little from what the bourgeois-democratic republics of the West have done to Versailles and Sanssouci. The Pushkin Museum Reserve in Mikhailovskoye or Tyutchev's house at Muranovo merely repeat in slightly altered, "Sovietized" form Goethe's house in Weimar and other Western memorial museum corners with their bourgeois cult of the individual.

[...]

11. Tribute should be paid to museum workers, especially rank-and-file museum staff, for their at times dedicated work, which has been quite thorough given the limits of their mindset. Its quality and results were largely due to the fact that for museum workers their service was their life's work. Of course, this is the best situation and, in principle, one worthy of emulation. However, it must be said that the people who have gone to work in museums have been the most apolitical people, people of the old mindset, people who have had nothing to do and have not wished to have anything to do with either the class struggle or the militant agenda. Museums and museum work have been, as it were, a way of escaping life, of choosing the least revolutionary, most old-fashioned corner in revolutionary reality.

[...]

13. Yet it is time to begin this revolution in the art museum field. The remoteness of museums from life, their historicism, have led to the fact that Marxist aesthetic thought has still not paid sufficient attention to them. "Agitated and hurriedly," the new, emergent Marxist art criticism has been defining its own basic theoretical and methodological positions, plunging headfirst into art journalism, and been wholly consumed in the struggle over the current state of contemporary visual art. This has also been necessary and right. But it is likewise right and inevitable that Marxist art criticism, now more or less firmly established and possessing certain new forces often more academically qualified than old museum staff, should seriously take up questions of museum development.

manufacturing aspect are considered only in terms of decorative, not structural problems. Even here there are no ordinary household objects, and the notion of the aesthetical is limited to decoration, that is, it revolves wholly within the bourgeois "applied arts" aesthetic.

34. Summarizing our critique of the exposition methods employed by our art museums, we come to the sad conclusion that they do not present the true historical process of art's evolution, but a fiction, that art is presented here in a subjective, unilateral, bourgeois-idealistic light. They preach the faith that bourgeois easel art is the only real, high, and outstanding art. Semi-easel or production art is presented in terms of easel art, moreover from the viewpoint of the highest affirmation of these principles in the decadent ideology of "art for art's sake." By showing art outside its social functions and relationships, its independence and "sacredness" is obliquely (albeit quite persuasively) proved. By showing rarities, idle curiosity, an unhealthy desire for the exotic and unusual, for an escape from real everyday life into the realm of deceptive mirages are encouraged. If our everyday life museum ensembles are quite often turned into an aesthetic apology for the squire's life, into a poeticization of serfdom, then our art museums are an apology for bourgeois art, a systematic and powerful inculcation of the foundations of bourgeois aesthetics in the minds of workers. In their contemporary state, art museums not only have no ties with the real political agenda of the day and fail to serve our building of socialism, but by virtue of their very structure and despite the rhetoric of tour guides, they affirm that such ties are impossible and unnecessary.

35. The system of structuring our art museums and the class nature of this system also impose their mark on cultural education and tours, sending them in the direction of the simplified culturalism that was discussed above. The selection of artifacts and the way they are displayed in art museums makes a genuinely Marxist interpretation of art nearly impossible while conducting tours. This is one of main obstacles in improving the sociological skills of our tour guides.
Instead of using the selection and display of material themselves to force viewers inevitably reach Marxist conclusions and valuations, the expositional method in our museums objectively hinders such attempts. The art material disputes the words of the guide, inevitably discredits them, and, of courses, emerges victorious in this struggle. This is one of the reasons that most of the anecdotal lapses usually adduced when criticizing the skills of our tour guides fall into the sociological and only rarely into the formal-aesthetic realm. Here, of course, the ideology of the tour guides - the school and system of views in which they were educated - makes itself known. I merely want to say that museum exposition methods not only fail to refashion this ideology of theirs, but, on the contrary, hinders its refashioning.

[...]

39. From the Marxist viewpoint, these responses are devoid of content; they are formal and bureaucratic. In certain of its parts, on closer examination so-called artistic culture may prove more harmful than helpful. Lacking in precisely determined class content, it is senseless; practically incompatible with our needs, it is a superfluous luxury.

40. What are the objectives and aims that derive from our understanding of culture, that our art museums must pursue, that should be the basis in reconstructing the art museum field? It seems to me that there are basically two such objectives, which determine the two main approaches to using material in art museums:
a. The task of teaching and scientifically demonstrating the basic laws and historical stages of social dynamics. Considered as a fact and factor of public life, in its everyday material and ideological significance, art is used as material, as document, as one graphic indicator among others of types of cultures, their internal structure, the dialectics of the class struggle in its various historical forms, of labor and economic history, and so on and so forth. Art is used as social science material. The practical aim is to educate conscious Soviet citizens, public activists, "managers of the state," active builders of socialism. This aim determines selection, classification, and all methods of display.
b. The task of studying art itself as such, its main types, historical periods, the sum of its basic tech-

niques and methods; the study and scientific demonstration of Marxist historical theory and its art-scholarly specificity. Here, the practical aims that determine the selection, classification, and display of art material are the real needs of contemporary operative art and advanced revolutionary aesthetic aspirations, and the conscious, systematic, scientifically grounded control of it to make it suitable for the needs of our time. Instead of the vague notion of raising the "artistic level," what is promoted is the problem of amateur art, defined as precisely as possible - awakening the desire amongst the worker-peasant masses to independently and creatively aestheticize their own daily lives.

41. In both types of museums, abstract historicism and learning the sum of historical facts should be replaced with the aim of mastering the nature and mechanism of phenomena, a mastery necessary for practical work.
Bourgeois thingism has led to a completely wrong approach to determining a museum's type on the basis of physical material: museums of painting, of porcelain, of furniture, of toys, and so on and so forth. This principle reveals its uselessness as soon as, alongside the tasks of simply collecting and displaying things for their own sake, the objectives of explaining them and, conversely, using them to explain real life processes are advanced. Thus, historical and historical everyday life museums, not being museums of some "material" or other, already claim to display all the things of material culture in general, including art objects. And this is completely correct, since from the scientific viewpoint a museum's type is determined not by the nature of the material, but by the approach to this material, as dictated by the museum's objectives.

[...]

43. In purely material terms, it would be extremely difficult to draw a line between art museums and the display of art in culture museums. In both cases, Marxist ideology will compel us not only to employ a complex exposition method but also to display not things, but processes. In both cases, art will be shown in its socio-economic nature; in both cases, diagrams, copies, and so on and so forth should be displayed next to the things. In both cases, the entire exposition oscillates between two poles: synthetic display of wholes as unities ("style," "type," etc.) and analytical decomposition into primary elements. But while it is difficult to employ the material principle in identifying the nature and content of art museums as opposed to other museums, within art museums themselves we will probably have to give up the division of art into genres. A museum's type can be derived solely from its objectives, just like the selection and juxtaposition of things; that is, the system of exposition can be determined and differentiated only by what needs to be proven, what aspect of a phenomenon has to be manifested.

[...]

45. As I have already noted, establishing the specific nature of the art museum is primarily a question of its methods of display.
The art museum and the culture museum have in common the display of art as a social phenomenon, as a fact of daily life. In terms of exposition, this affinity is due to common methods of complex display. What is the peculiarity of complex artistic display compared with historical display? First of all, of course, it by no means has anything to do with proverbial "artiness," that is, with aestheticizing. By itself, a complex display is no salvation and does not require a materialist, Marxist approach to phenomena. A simple combination of architecture, sculpture, painting, and mass-produced art does not generate the "functional" exposition I discussed earlier. There still remains, in this case, the abstract visual approach nurtured on easel painting and promoted by our art museums nowadays. In such assemblages, there is always the danger of drifting into so-called art-and-everyday-life ensembles, which are the worst kind of aestheticism, since not only is art not interpreted in this case through its social functions, but also, on the contrary, all of history is artificially aestheticized. A particular period is transformed, here, into a magically captivating romance or a petit-bourgeois aesthetic lollipop.[6] Examples are plentiful. Such are all our country estate museums, monastery museums, "houses of the 1840s," and so on and so forth.

46. Given the ambiguity of the term "art," it would be more cor-

rect to speak of the type not of the art but of the art scholarship museum. This would, in principle, once and for all sweep aside all aesthetic approaches and produce a specification based not on the hidden tendency to oppose science and art, but on the tendency to establish the specificity of the art scholarship sector as part of the unified system of the scientific approach to the world. The art scholarship museum would thus resemble the cultural museum to the extent that art scholarship employs the historical method and is part of the science of culture. And, on the contrary, the extent of its specificity would be defined by the scope of the special problems addressed by contemporary advanced art scholarship.

[...]

48. The art scholarship museum should ideally be an expanded sociology of art visualized in artifacts. The transitional stage is the museum of art history constructed according to Marxist principles.

[...]

51. In capitalist society, architecture and mass-produced art are superficially decorative and applied arts. The museums of the former Stieglitz and Stroganov academies were collections of exemplars from all periods, nations, and styles, and these were meant to be eclectically emulated. For us nowadays, this emulation is no longer suitable: we want to create a new organic style, whose essence would not be superficial decoration but constructive form-creation, the most perfect, practicable, and high-quality design of objects. Accordingly, so-called museums of decorative art are also unacceptable and harmful to us in their present state.
When people say nowadays that the Porcelain Museum or Furniture Museum contributes to increasing the "artistry" of our porcelain and woodworking industry, then what they mean by "artistry" is the stupid Sovietization of petit-bourgeois stylizations of various sorts. A "Soviet Empire style" and "Soviet Russian style," with hammers and sickles instead of eagles and roosters, are the only things to which museums of decorative art in their present state can lead a factory draftsman.

52. We know that Brunelleschi and Michelangelo were great architects because they were the greatest structural engineers of their time. We know that a medieval carver or Benvenuto Cellini were the best craftsmen of their ages, that they knew and understood their material and their tasks, that they transformed its hidden possibilities into artistic reality. Learning from these masters does not mean repeating their language of forms, but understanding their system of techniques, their artistic methodology and technology. The "testament" and teaching of any major style and master can only amount to one thing: to pursuing a given objective in the most optimal way given the material and conditions of artistic production.

53. It is thus clear that an art education museum should in no case be a museum of "styles," a museum of artistic exemplars. It shows not things, but processes of production, the technique and technology of art. It decomposes the complex phenomenon of art into primary, irreducible material-formal elements and demonstrates possible systems for combining them. Familiarizing him with the technology of materials and the functional emergence of artistic form, it gives the artist/craftsman only the opportunity to convert his ideas into artistic facts, without crushing him under the heavy burden of dead aesthetic traditions.

54. The term "art scholarship museum," while it has its advantages, requires some clarification, however. We should in no way imagine that it denotes a museum for art scholars, a museum with a narrow and specific meaning, and that I thus propose turning art museums from scientific and educational institutions into purely scientific, ancillary facilities. It seems to me entirely correct that Narkompros recently adopted the position that museums are primarily scientific and educational institutions. This is all the more correct in that for Marxists there is no contradiction between science and the popularization of science, between research and education. On the one hand, any scientific theory can be popularized. On the other, as Lenin correctly pointed out, popularization should in no way amount to vulgarization: the laboring masses must be given the entirety of science in accessible form, moreover, via its latest, highest achievements.

55. The contradiction between science and education, which exists

in the system of bourgeois culture and is felt most strongly in the so-called humanities, is due to the separation of these sciences from social practice, to their focus on themselves as ends and values in themselves. "Pure science for science's sake" is the fruit of armchair individualism and is speculative by nature. On the contrary, the "art scholarship museum" I am proposing is based on the problems of artistic practice, is conditioned by them, and finds its specificity in the properly formulated aesthetic education of the masses. The issue of the possibility or impossibility of a purely aesthetic, pleasure-oriented appreciation of art in museums of the new type thus also becomes clear.

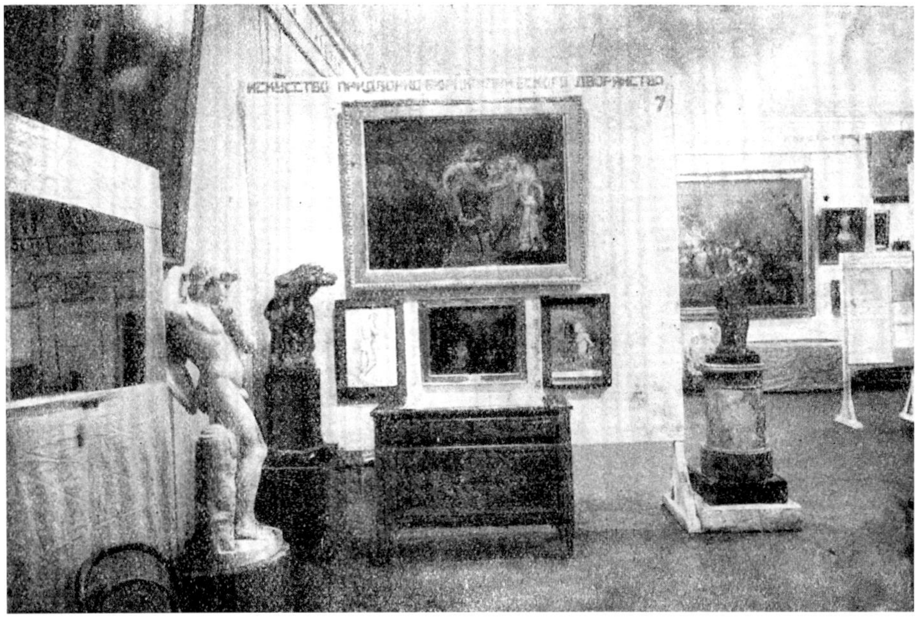

56. Having established the bourgeois nature of art museums as a particular historical category, it is theoretically possible to conclude that they must be replaced with purely scientific art museums. But to demand the cessation of aesthetic educational work in museums right now would be pointless, as the aesthetic value of museums can only wither away, along with the aesthetic that gave rise to museums, when works of bourgeois art ceased to be appreciated aesthetically. But this will happen only after the destruction of money-commodity relations in art. The masses go to art museums not only to be educated but also to admire art for the simple reason that they lack this art in life. This role of museums will continue to diminish proportionally as art is introduced into life, on the one hand, by placing works of easel art in clubs and public places; on the other, by replacing easel forms of visual art with other forms of it and by developing amateur art.

57. It is completely clear that aesthetic appreciation is also possible in the art scholarship-type museum, not to mention the transitional stages to this type of museum. After all, artworks remain safe and sound in such museums; the scientific arrangement and presentation of these works in no way prevents the possibility of appreciating them aesthetically. It is time to drop the old idealist dichotomy between science and art, according to which aesthetic experience is deemed irrational and somehow unconscious.

58. As concerns the aesthetic education of the masses, not only has it not been eliminated or forgotten, but, as I have repeatedly emphasized, it is the basis of the art scholarship museum. But aesthetic education does not necessarily involve only the irrational appreciation of art, only awe, admiration, and wonder. The idealists who oppose science and art will never risk taking their thoughts to their logical conclusions, as they would then have to admit that the art museum is not a scientific and educational institution, but should be a "temple of art," a place for aesthetic zealotry. They do not dare to say this, but they understand and structure aesthetic education in terms contrary to science. As I have said, the point here is that they want to educate the proletariat not only on bourgeois art but using bourgeois methods. For them, aesthetic education is limited to its bourgeois conception, just as their notion of art is limited to easel art.

59. In fact, if, to the extent that there is still a demand for easel art (that is, art that is bourgeois in terms of economics and production), the inheritance of old museum art can and must be used aesthetically, then in using it, we must criticize it, show its true nature and meaning; not praise it to the heavens, but show that even in

its supreme achievements it was weak in comparison with the liberated and technically enriched art of the future. If it is useful for the contemporary artist to learn a thing or two from the old masters, on the other hand by this very teaching and promotion of the old art's supreme specimens we support easel art, which is doomed to destruction. Along with the use of easel art as a positive factor for the present period, we must promote other types of visual art and juxtapose them to easel forms by way of revealing the relative nature and historical and class limitations of the latter. It is thus completely clear that the question of aesthetic education, of the aesthetic use of the museum, is a tactical question, and its content is determined by the specific objectives of artistic policy, which need not be expounded here. It only bears saying that in using the old aesthetic inheritance for the needs of today, the museum must structure its aesthetic educational work so as not to preserve remnants of the old culture, but to encourage the buds of the new.

[...]

61. Given the new direction in understanding the nature and objectives of art museums, we must recognize that the national-territorial criterion for dividing material is unsound as the primary criterion of classification. With the gradual transition from the historically oriented type of art museum to the sociologically oriented type, we must shift from a chronological arrangement of material to a typological arrangement.

[...]

63. As we struggle with contemporary museum expositional methods, we need to combat with their "monumental" staticness. Museums must cease to be enormous frozen organizations, almost incapable of evolution and movement. Permanent exhibitions should more and more give way to temporary exhibitions, to different expositional experiments. The material a museum has on display should be in constant flux.
We are currently still quite poor, and our museums are housed, perhaps, in quite "artistic" buildings, but they are ill suited to the new type of museums. When constructing new museum buildings, it will be necessary to address the question of mechanizing museums (movable hanging rods, floors, and partitions), which will make it much easier to deal with the problem of dynamic museum display. But as a principle, it should be acknowledged now, because without it no reorganization of our art museums is possible.

64. My article will provoke, of course, a good deal of indignation and opposition from all manner of priests and guardians. Therefore, in conclusion, I would like to specifically make it clear that:
a. I am not calling for the destruction of the valuable art of the past nor I do deny art as a specific sphere of public life. I am merely combating the fetishization of art objects, their substitution for the living flux of art, and the stranglehold of aestheticized enthusiastic art appreciation to the detriment of objectively scientific study, seeing it as a manifestation of an alien, hostile ideology.
b. I do not propose destroying art museums in general nor do I deny the possibility and necessity of the existence of such museums. I only argue that their specificity is defined not by their material, but by their object of study, not by the sum of things they house, but by the sum of approaches they employ.

65. I am least of all a dreamer and I clearly recognize the slim opportunities at present for practically implementing the radical reorganization of art museums into the art scholarship museums discussed above. Not only a "sociological" but even a genuinely scientific "historical" approach is extremely difficult to effectuate in our museums at present. There are neither the forces nor the necessary cadres of young fresh workers for this, and too great is the power of the old aesthetic tradition, of the intelligentsia's sensual, quasireligious attitude to art, and so on and so forth.

66. But the practical near-impossibility of implementing this cannot be an obstacle to posing the question theoretically in all its fundamental purity and clear logical acuteness.

67. The minimal practical measures that can and must be taken now, at this stage of the cultural revolution, include:
a. Studying and reorganizing the museum network, moreover not bureaucratically, but in terms of research. Creating a rationally structured museum network, corresponding to the political, eco-

nomic, and socio-cultural regionalization of the USSR.
Turning the semi-spontaneous process of organizing new local museums into planned museum development.
b. In keeping with this reorganization of the museum network, carrying out a maximally broad redistribution of museum materials. Decreasing the size of the enormous central museums, and increasing and systematizing at their expense the collections of museums in the most important provincial cities. Destroying the "property rights" of certain museums to their collections.
c. Partial tests of new exposition methods, based on the new understanding of art museums and relying on Marxist art criticism. Experimental gallery spaces must be allocated in all museums; an experimental laboratory museum station should be established that would coordinate and direct the experimental work of museums. This work should aim to pursue practical objectives both in the field of art and in social and political life.
d. A definite shift from exhibitions organized according to artist (in picture galleries) and factory (in so-called decorative museums) to exhibitions organized, at very least, by style, as established by advanced bourgeois art scholarship.
e. Destroying the insularity and "independence" of museums, their separation from art and educational institutions.

Originally published in the journal *Press and Revolution*, no. 4, April 1929, pp. 63-79.

[1] A perfect example is the recent story of the production of counterfeit Donatellos in Italy.
[2] These casts owe their origin to the fact that the Museum of Fine Arts was originally built as a teaching museum of Moscow University.
[3] Now, when a number of new workers have been infused in the Tretyakov State Gallery, measures for remedying this shortcoming have been taken, and work on new exhibits is underway as well.
[4] This, of course, does not mean that bourgeois aesthetics actually treats with equal attention and interest all periods of the history of art and the artistic ideology of different classes at different stages of evolution. Bourgeois aesthetics is essentially subjective and limited, like any classist aesthetics, but consciously and theoretically it aspires to be objective. We see something quite analogous in the discipline of history, where a classist interpretation of history is passed off as if it were objectively dispassionate. This contradiction is characteristic of all bourgeois ideology and is due to the bourgeoisie's need to conceal the limitedness and narrowness of its ideals out of social and political considerations.
[5] Cf. E.K. Kverfeld, *Artistic Woodworking Techniques*, Leningrad, Museum of the Society for the Advancement of the Arts, 1928.
[6] "Because there is no authentic everyday life in the staterooms of these palaces and mansions, but only a gilded frame in which this life's ceremonial side once flowed, this reception can be painted before the visitor's eyes, in this frame, in this picture of a fairy-tale life, a life of supreme beauty and inexhaustible elegance: it was good to live in that magical time! Although the authentic everyday life of the period, apprehended not through the things in the staterooms, but easily reproducible via plentiful categories of other sources, would horrify us now, including in these palaces and mansions, in terms of the rudeness of its manners, which we have left far behind along with the abolition of slavery, in terms of the stuffiness and dirtiness of its everyday customs, which we, in the age of indoor plumbing, electricity, and personal cleanliness as a mass phenomenon, would find it simply hard to imagine." Mikhail Dmitrievich Priselkov, *Historical-Everyday Life Museums*, Leningrad 1926, p. 5.

The Places of History

Arseniy Zhilyaev

Since Baudelaire's time, the artist has been imagined as someone rooted in the tradition of overcoming tradition. Artists have been obliged to keep abreast of fashion and spend their time in endless *flânerie*, thus resisting being stopped or captured in space. In the twentieth century, the public figure or activist was primarily a revolutionary, an adherent of the tradition of combating tyranny; at the extreme, an adept of permanent revolution. He or she fought against the limitations imposed by time, by specific historical periods, and this struggle was waged on behalf of a utopian future. The Bolshevik Trotsky wrote that he was always rooted in a tradition, but this tradition was called revolution.

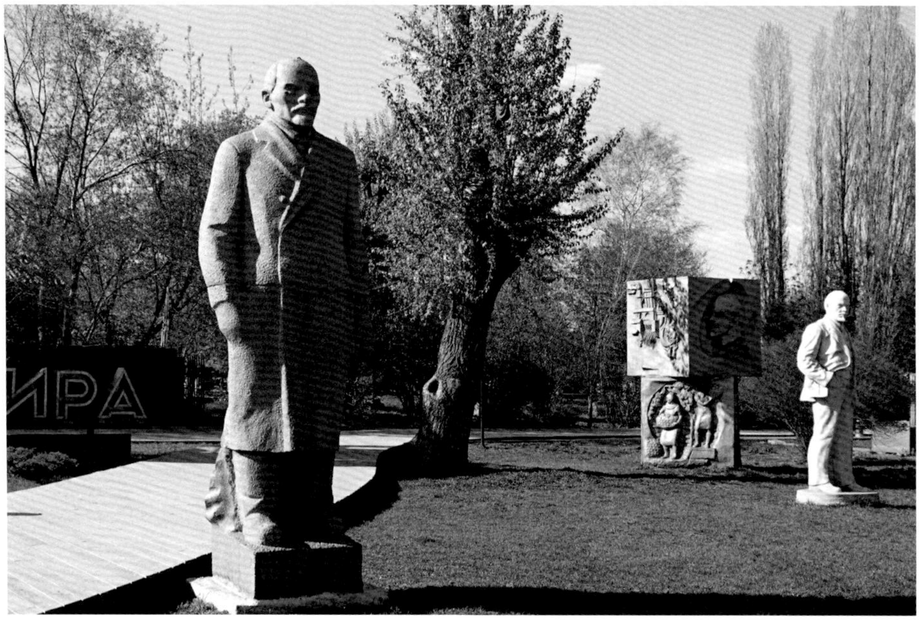

The museum of the revolution and the museum of modernist art are meeting places for the politician and the artist fighting against the limitations of time and space; they are heterotopias that have paradoxically retained their importance despite the radicalism of certain twentieth-century thinkers who were opposed to any spatio-temporal capture. The discourse around the museum's status in the twentieth century was essentially a discussion of the limits of emancipatory projects. It simultaneously pointed to the possibility that an imaginary future could exist in a special way in the "here and now" of museum space, which resembles other heterotopias identified by Foucault, for example, the cemetery. And indeed, it is still assumed that capturing or recording any phenomenon (whether an event of public life or of art) in words or by placing it in a museum is tantamount to its death. Clearly aware of this relationship, many members of the historical avant-garde called for the destruction of museums: "Stop showing dead artists!" In many respects, however, it has in fact been the extreme materialism of the museum, whose existence is focused on things – artifacts possessed of artistic significance or documentary evidence of revolutionary struggle – that has indicated the impossibility of overcoming the museum in the modern world. The museum manifests a particular form of life after death. The desire to reset history, a perpetual tarrying at the zero point, itself begins to produce its own history. And perhaps this type of life is, paradoxically, one of the few means of experiencing history as such.

***

To identify the museum's main theme, the lobby should be designed as a narrative of the central event of the Revolution of 1905, the December armed uprising.

«The exploit of the Presnya workers was not useless. Their sacrifices were not in vain. The first breach was made in the edifice of the tsarist monarchy, a breach that slowly but steadily grew wider and undermined the old and medieval order.»
V.I. Lenin, *Letter to Workers of Red Presnya District of Moscow*, December 25, 1920, *Collected Works*, Vol. 31, 4th English Edition, Moscow, Progress Publishers, p. 535.

Ivan Shadr's sculpture *The Cobblestone Is the Weapon of the Proletariat* or another sculptural group.

The glass bays should be decorated with motifs invoking the fighting on the barricades in Presnya. Various artistic media can be used: color photographs, drawings on glass, colored mosaics etc.

V.I. Lenin, 1891. Photograph
***

Structurally, the musem has to exit time and space to occupy a meta-position that would preserve stability, on the one hand, while also being maximally filled with volatile content. The very intention of displaying revolution or modernist art in the museum is extremely contradictory. Resisting contraction into a single image, revolution is, rather, an example of interrupting the historical narrative, of a sublime, un*imag*inable experience (in the sense of being unamenable to capture in images). However, we know that there exists an extensive stock of images of revolution. The same can be said of modernist art, which is designed to capture the death of art again and again. The museum operates in a specific way. It cannot claim to reveal the entire history of life or art. On the contrary, its deliberate insufficiency underwrites a full experience of history. As in the religious tradition, where aphophatic expressions indicate the divine presence through negation, the museum points to historical experience itself through an obsessive, sometimes grotesque, exaggerated and simplified representation of the history of revolution (whether in aesthetics or politics). Just think: can a mammoth's bone really invoke in us the complex experience of humanity's millenia-long struggle for survival? We can have this experience only by recognizing the bone's extreme insignificance compared with the mass of matter that has undergone countless metamorphoses over that time. And Hitler's towel? The fact that the villain was a simple man of flesh and blood only throws into starker relief Hitler's deeds as a historical person.

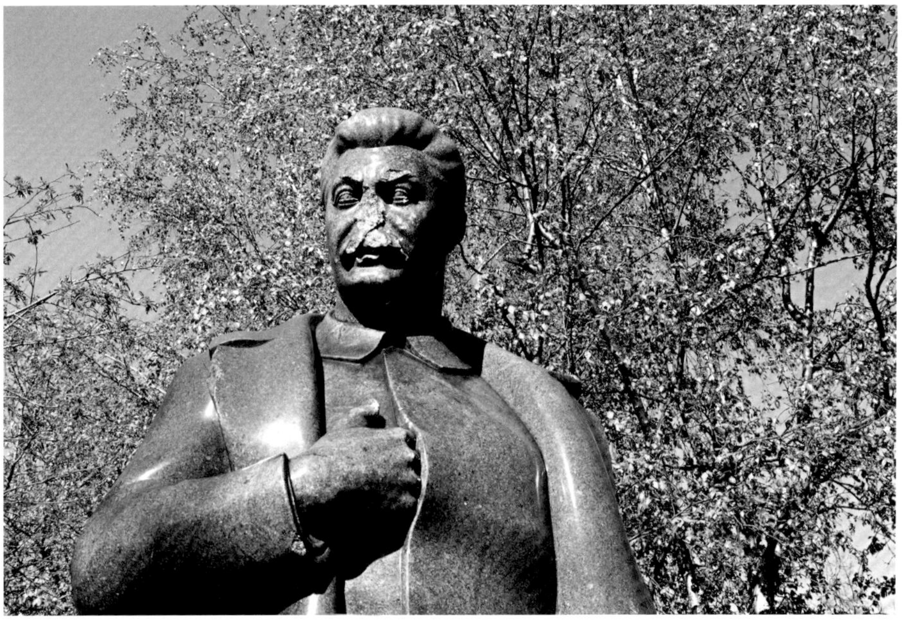

***
«[I]n the nineties two profound social movements converged in Russia: one, a spontaneous movement, a popular movement within the working class, the other, the movement of social thought in the direction of the theory of Marx and Engels, towards the theory of Social-Democracy.» V.I. Lenin, *A Retrograde Trend in Russian Social-Democracy*, *Collected Works*, Vol. 4, Moscow, Progress Publishers, 1964, pp. 255-285.

N.A. Kasatkin, *Strike*. Pen and ink drawing

Report by an industrial inspector at the Prokhorov Factory on illegal meetings of workers there. November 23, 1895. Photocopy
***

After the thirties, Soviet official art no longer thematizes this gap, this interruption in tradition. It becomes part of everyday life and as such rightfully enters historical museums and, of course, museums of the revolution, but only as an ancillary part of the exhibition that is not entirely a work of art but is suspended, rather, between scholarship, art, and everyday life. In any case, that was how it was supposed to be, if we take into account the views of the Marxist experimenters in museology, who subordinated all material artifacts and art objects to an academic historical narrative about the struggle for the emancipation of the oppressed classes. At the same time, by virtue of its specific status, the museum of the revolution could exist only as an artistic and scholarly project: it was not intended to reflect the public life of post-revolutionary society in its entirety. The image of the revolution was presented from a biased position, the position of the Party: here there could be no "objectivity," as understood as the fullness and pluralism of the bourgeois museum of modernism. Moreover, the revolution, the sacred moment when Soviet history emerged, could find no other place in this history aside from the place of a revered idol that had forfeited its power. The

Stalinist concept of museology dictated that the revolution should be situated in a strict institutional framework. Its character, sublime and resisting all capture, had to be reduced to a pretty, easily assimilable mythological narrative. This was the principal anti-modernist artistic conceit of Soviet museology. But for these same reasons the role of the conceptual artist was so important. He or she was an artist/curator capable of building the heterotopia of the museum of the revolution, of constructing a historical narrative about the interruption of the historical narrative, in other words, someone capable of fashioning an image of the revolution.

If we are looking for the socialist version of modernist art, the socialist version of the modernist museum, then it ought to be the museum of the revolution that we find. Paradoxically, despite all the conceptual differences, the museum of the revolution, when examined from the viewpoint of art, exhibits all the distinctive features of modernism – the institutional attachment and containment within the museum building – as opposed to the avant-garde's set towards smashing the borders between art and life.

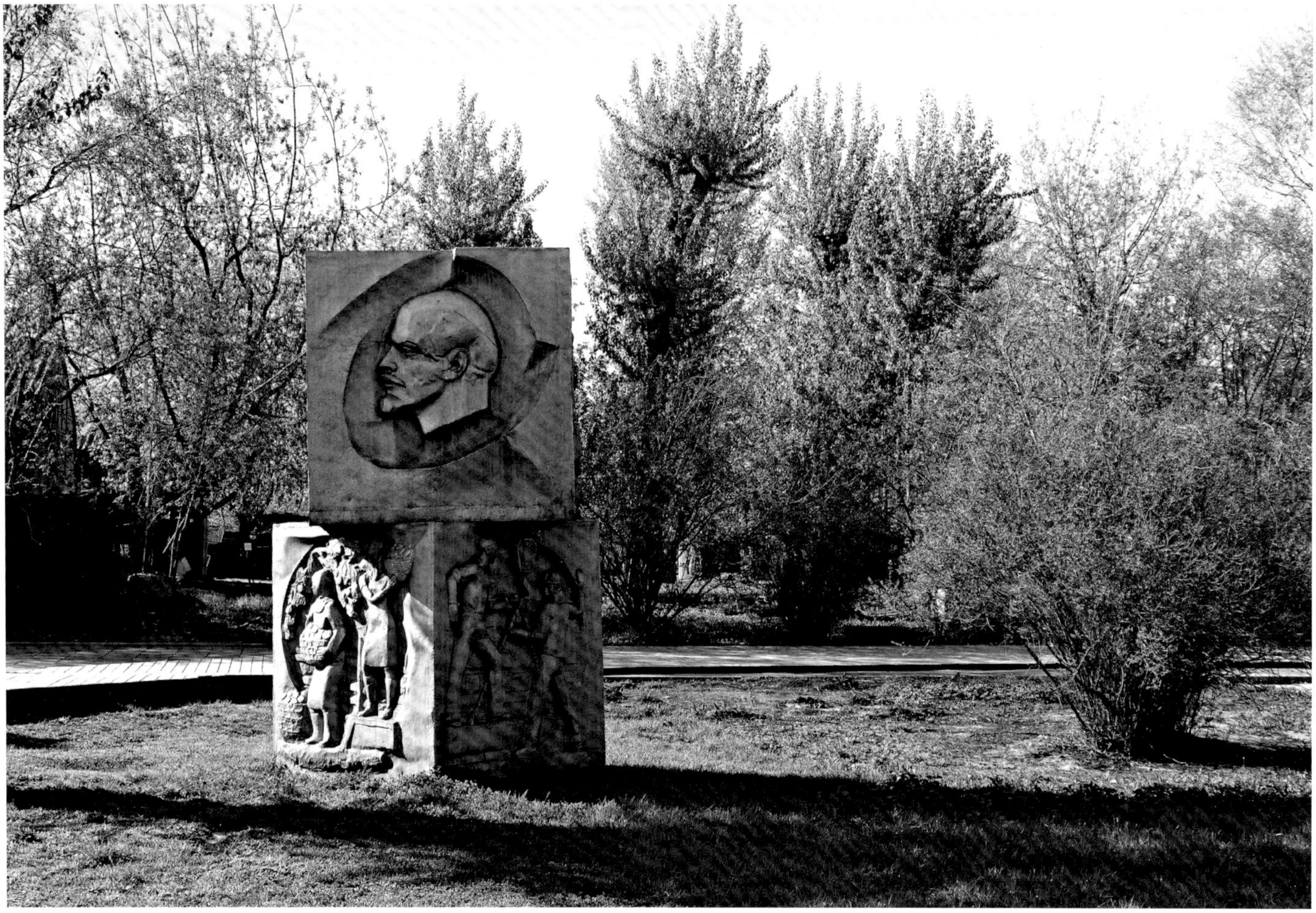

***

Activities of the Moscow Workers' Union, 1894-1898. Connections with industrial enterprises in Moscow. Diagram

Active members of the Moscow Workers' Union. Photomontage

a. M.N. Lyadov
b. S.I. Mickiewiz
c. A.N. Vinokurov
d. M.F. Vladimirovsky
e. E.I. Sponti
f. S.I. Prokofiev
g. P.I. Vinokurova
h. V.V. Vorovsky
i. A.I. Ulyanova

***

Most of modernist art's radical democratic aspirations were already realized in laboratory form in Soviet museums in the twenties. And here it was primarily a matter of artistically visualizing the radical break with tradition, of overcoming the gap between viewer and artist. Immediately after the revolution, Soviet museums carried out a controversial experiment in involving workers in their activities. The abandonment of the pictorial genre, which engages only the eye, in favor of installation art, which involves the entire human body, was proclaimed. Attempts were made to overcome the hierarchical relationship between copy and original. The creators of the first "ambient scenes" (which were essentially sculptural installations) eschewed authenticity in their choice of materials: pride of place was given to the historical narrative, which in turn defetishized the museum artifacts with which the nineteen-century bourgeois museum had been filled. Like modernist art, Soviet museum installations claimed to be scientific. The museum narrative was based on the Marxist interpretation of history, while the exposition was arranged with the psychological features of human perception in mind. Finally, like the best specimens of modernist art, Soviet museums strongly criticized speculative effects in the service of ideology. Museums of atheism, which laid bare the mechanisms of producing miracles for believers, can be regarded as the highest achievement of this kind. In general, exhibitions in these museums provoked a critical attitude toward the production of spectacles: an abundance of texts, statistics, and other food for thought prevented the viewer from dissolving in the aesthetic experience. Their mode of functioning was congenial to what, a short while later, the world would come to know as Bertolt Brecht's interpretation of realism. By its very nature, the installation-based museum space cannot be regarded as an illusionistic space. Its essential organizational principle is the collage, although the collage's elements are subordinated to the overall storyline. At the same time, the museum of the revolution remained close to the avant-garde tradition. This was mainly reflected in the collective creativity practiced by the creators of the exhibitions, on the one hand, and the claim to the nonartistic character of their ventures. Museum exhibitions were not seen as artistic statements, and as a rule the names of their creators were not officially included in their titles. And unlike the modernist museum, the museum of the revolution provided an example of human freedom embodied in the space of society rather than the space of institutional aesthetics.

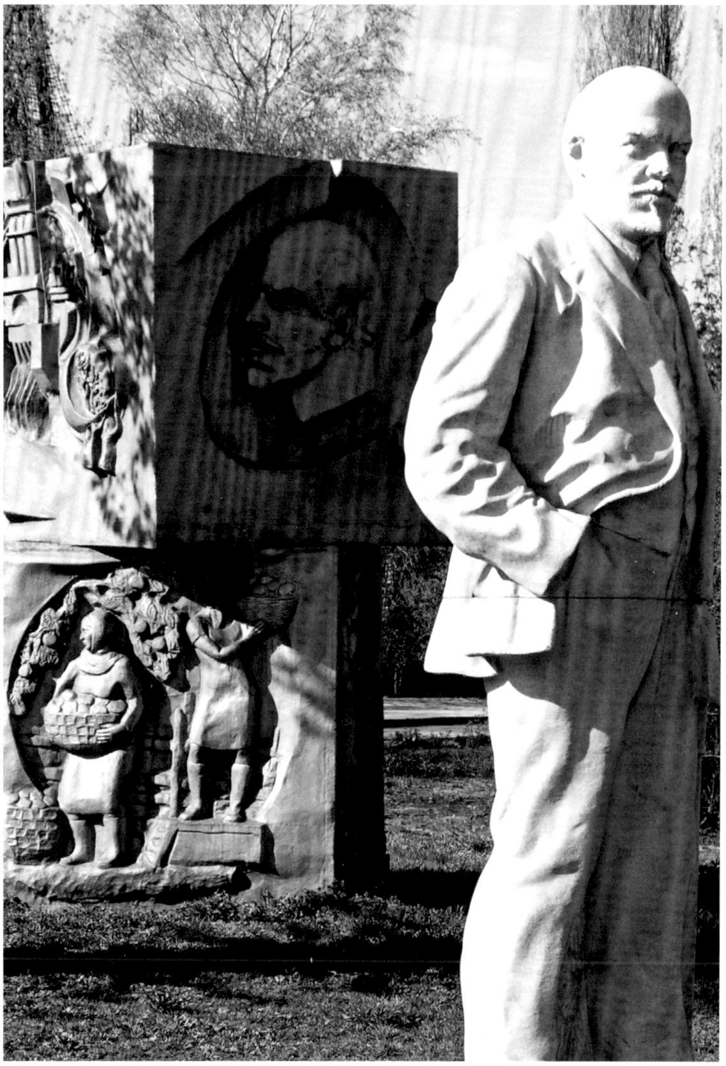

***

Report by the Moscow Okhrana, dated November 10, 1896, on a strike by 400 workers in the workshops of the Moscow-Brest Railway. Central State Archive of the City of Moscow, f. 16, op. 86, ed. khr. 121, l. 46. Photocopy of original document

List of workers at the Prokhorov Factory, arrested on January 28 and 29, 1898, for involvement in a strike. Photocopy of original document

***

The relationship between the modernist museum and the museum of the revolution can be examined through Boris Groys's schematic for understanding the relationship between the curatorial installation and the artist-produced installation. Whereas the curatorial installation, according to Groys, corresponds to institutional freedom, and the curator is obliged to publicly justify the exhibition concept to civil society, the artist installation corresponds to sovereign freedom, which has no need whatsoever to justify itself. The tension between these two poles characterizes the attitude towards freedom within bourgeois democracy, where sovereign freedom explicitly extends to consumption, religion, and behavior in personal space, and to things that pose no direct threat to the prevailing order. Everything else is up for discussion, at best. Consequently, projects that play on the relationship between these two modes of artistically organizing space possess a demystifying, critical potential that exposes the mechanisms for the production of hegemony in the western world.

The modernist museum is the classic example of the curatorial installation. Viewers find themselves in a maximally neutral, white space where the curator shows them specimens of individual, creative, sovereign freedom, united by a concept acceptable from the viewpoint of institutional freedom (that is, from the viewpoint of the ruling class). The museum of the revolution is an example of an artistic installation, produced by a collective proletarian creator, the possesser of sovereign freedom. Following Groys's thought, the curatorial installation ideally assumes the presence of a collective viewer. This collective viewer has great emancipatory potential, as it is free from history and any social obligations whatsoever. This viewer, however, is unaware of itself and therefore cannot actualize this potential.

Like modernist art, capitalist society exists in a mode of permanent crisis. It constantly revolutionizes pre-capitalist systems of relations and its own internal contradictions, so its habitual state is an indefinite extension of the end of history. In popular culture, this is reflected in constant expectation of the apocalypse. By contrast, viewers at the museum of the revolution are rooted in the moment of history's beginning, whose collective subject includes both them and the exhibition's creators. The space where Soviet artists manifested their sovereign will merged with the public space where popular culture was produced. Ideally, class collective will and individual artistic will, directed towards establishing a new, just, democratic society based on equality, should have converged in this place. It is here that the creative imagination, among other things, gives rise to what in its utopian version could be envisioned as a total work of art produced by a society freed from oppression.

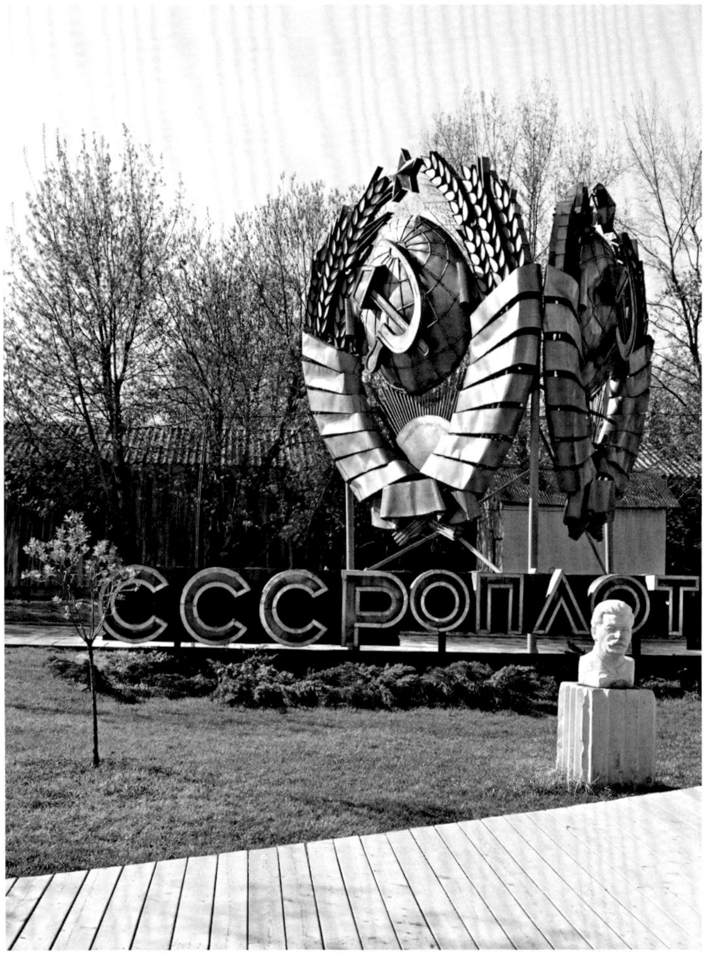

***

Organizers of Marxist circles in the industrial enterprises of Presyna, February 1894. Photomontage

a. E.I. Nemchinov, worker at the Brest Railway workshops, member of the Workers' Union, member of the circle at the Brest Railway worskhops.
b. F.I. Polyakov, worker and member of the Workers' Union, organizer of workers' circles at the Prokhorov Factory and other textile enterprises in Moscow.
c. K.F. Boyer, worker at the Weiheld Factory and member of the Workers' Union.

"They Parleyed at the Factory Inspector's Office," one of the first leaflets of the Moscow Workers' Union, February 1894. Photocopy
"Comrade Workers!," a leaflet issued by the Moscow Workers' Union, 1894. Photocopy

S.S. Boym, *First Illegal May Day Meeting in Moscow, 1895.* Painting
***

Beside the museum of modern art and the museum of the revolution, where else can a person come face to face with history? Or is the paradoxical life after death we find in the heterotopia the only mode of existence in late capitalism? I would also include among such places the urban spaces where today's protesters fight for their rights. The method of the Occupy Wall Street movement is quite similar to the practices developed by museum curators: physically inserting into a dead place, which nevertheless has the potential to produce emancipatory history, what is alive today and capable of actualizing this historic potential. Whether we like it or not, political action in today's world still requires physical, bodily presence. This fact, so painful for the Facebook generation, essentially defines the formula of the political today. "Copy, paste, go offline": this is the three-move combination that links aspirations for the future with the here and now of a particular public place. Only physical presence enables communication in the mass demonstration mode. This demand sometimes goes to almost religious extremes, a good example being the practice of the "mic check."

In the case of political action, the question of physical presence is the key, especially when it comes to "terrorist acts." It is physical presence in a specific place that poses the greatest threat to the current authorities. Place as the potential for material presence is the basis of future history and, therefore, of power. Aggression by authorities towards people who are merely present in a park next to a stock exchange is surprising, although for someone acquainted with the history of twentieth-century art there is much that is familiar in this aggression. No matter what a thing was before it ended up in the modernist museum, it was liberated there from all functional limitations and acquired the untouchable status of an artwork. The central question, which remains open, is whether current liberation movements can make the transition from the modernist museum's institutional freedom to the museum of the revolution's sovereign freedom.

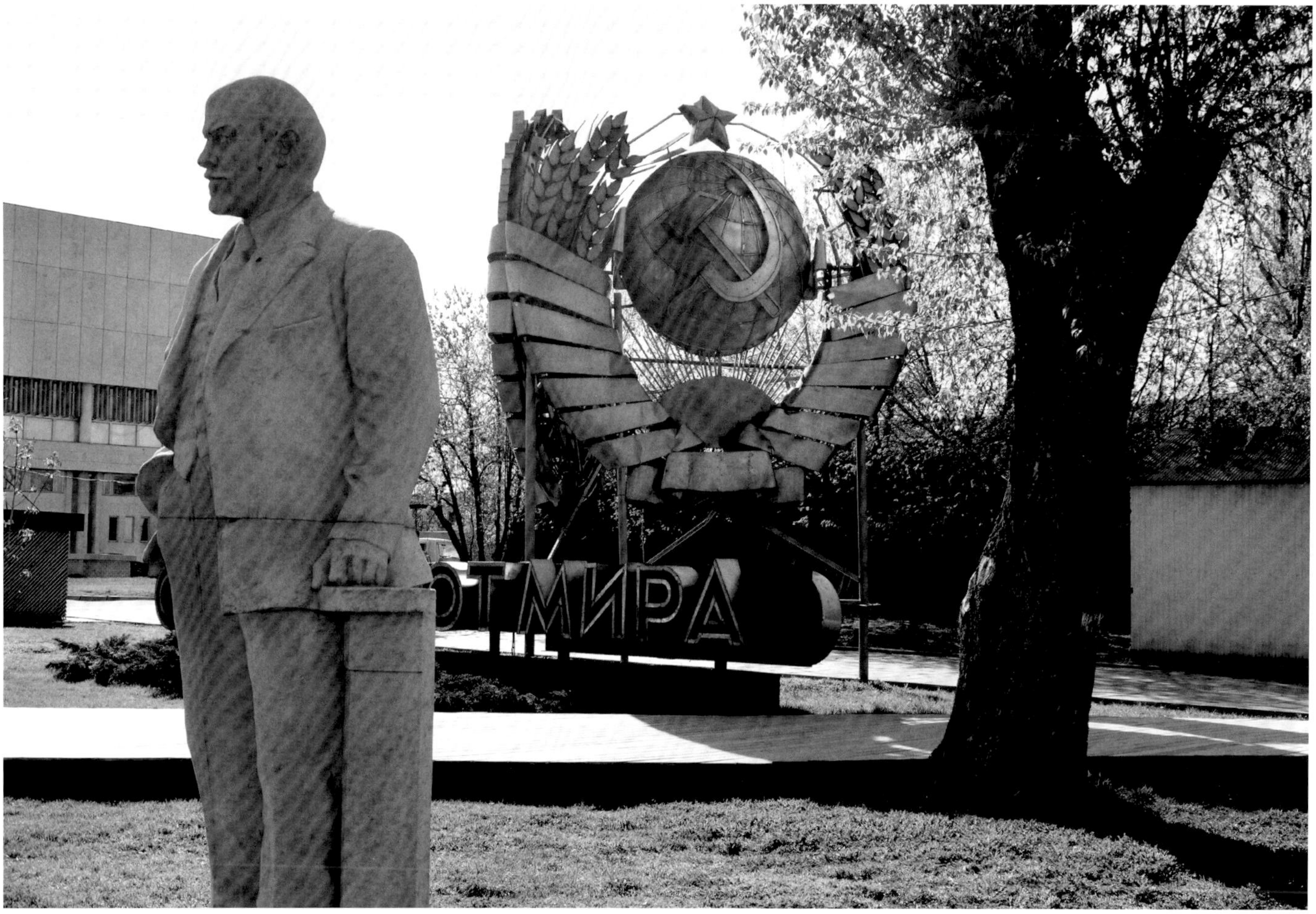

The parts marked by *** in this text are taken from a handwritten curatorial book with the description of an exhibition held at the *Museum of 1905 Revolution* (today *Historical and Memorial Museum "Presnya"*). The book was written to represent the exhibition to directors and censors in the late 1980s.

Arseniy Zhilyaev (born in 1984 in Voronezh, Russia) is an artist, writer and political activist who lives and works in Moscow. Zhilyaev's artistic practice poses questions about the cultural production in the postsoviet condition. Whithin his most recent projects: the *Museum of Proletarian Culture* (Tetryakov State Gallery, Moscow, 2012), *Pedagogical Poem* (Presnya Historical Memorial Museum, Moscow, 2012), *Radio October* (Proekt Fabrika, 2010). Zhilyaev is the winner of the *Innovation 2010* state award in the sphere of contemporary art and of the *Soratnik 2010* and *Soratnik 2012* (*Companion-in-Arms*) award.

SOLO EXHIBITIONS

2012
Museum of Proletarian Culture. The Industrialization of Bohemia, Tretyakov State Gallery, Moscow
Pedagogical poem (with Iliya Budraytskis and collective of authors), Presnya museum, Moscow

2011
Radio "October", Project Fabric, Moscow

2010
Rational egoism, Regina gallery, Moscow
New museum of revolution, HLAM, Voronezh, Russia

GROUP EXHIBITIONS

2013
Disobedience Archive (The Republic), Castello di Rivoli Museo d'Arte Contemporanea, Turin, Italy

2012
The Way of Enthusiasts, Casa dei Tre Oci, Venice, Italy
Under a Tinsel Sun, main project of Moscow International Biennale for Young Art, CHOA, Moscow, Russia
Génération P, Festival RussenKo, Le Kremlin-Bicêtre, France

2011
Once Upon a Present, Gallery SC, Zagreb, Croatia
Nuts, Regina gallery, London, England
In search of an alternative, East by South West, Galerie Grita Insam, Vienna, Austria
Practice everyday life, Calvert 22, London, England
Phantom monuments, Art Centre Garage, Moscow, Russia

2010
Interpolare, KJDT, Vienna, Austria
Prigov: point of construction, NCCA, Moscow, Russia
Vis a vis, Ecole nationale des beaux-arts de Lyon, France
Modernikon. Contemporary Art from Russia, Fondazione Sandretto Re Rebaudengo, Turin, Italy
Histoy lesson, Palais de Tokio, Paris, France
FQ-Test, GMG, Moscow, Russia
Russian utopias, Art Centre Garage, Moscow, Russia
Open doors day, MMOMA, Moscow, Russia

SELECTED BIBLIOGRAPHY

A. Shental, *Discursive Interventions into Russian Art*, Frieze blog, January, 31, 2013, http://blog.frieze.com/discursive-interventions-into-russian-art/
S. Franceschini, *Artists at Work: Arseniy Zhilyaev*, in *Afterall*, November, 21, 2012, http://www.afterall.org/online/artists-at-work-arseniy-zhilyaev
L. McLean-Ferris, *A practice of everyday life: Young Artists from Russia*, in *The Independent*, March, 30, 2011
E. Degot, *A new order*, in *Artforum*, November 2010
La machine de l'eches, Rue Descartes, #69
I. Calderoni, *Quando la forma è sovversiva. L'arte russa è un carrarmato*, in *l'Unità*, September, 23, 2010

MARIA CHEKHONADSKIH

Theoretician, curator, activist. Born in Stary Oskol, USSR in 1985, she graduated from Voronezh State University, Philosophical Faculty in Cultural Studies in 2007. In 2009 she obtained her MA in Cultural Studies at the Russian State University of the Humanities. She is now a PhD student at Kingston University, CRMEP (London). She has been Editor of the *Moscow Art Magazine* (*Khudozhestvennyi zhurnal*) since 2009. As a researcher and activist she is involved in intense debates around precarity. Her PhD thesis is based on the philosophical problematization of precarity in the context of Diderot, Hegel and Marx's discussions about class and modes of subjectivation within the capitalist production. Her curatorial approach is based on micro-analyzes of historical and anthropological problems such as precarity, daily life and social imagination. Her more recent projects include *Care*, a land art project (Voronezh-Moscow 2009-2010) and *Precarious Life* (Moscow, 2011). She is currently working on a new exhibition project entitled *Understanding Conspiracy* together with historian and artist Ilya Budraytskis. Her texts have been published in *Moscow Art Magazine*, *Radical Philosophy*, *Mediation*, *Alfabeta2*.

NICHOLAS CULLINAN

Curator of Modern and Contemporary Art at The Metropolitan Museum of Art in New York. He holds his BA, MA and PhD from the Courtauld Institute of Art. Before joining the Met, he was Curator of International Modern Art at the Tate Modern in London, where he worked on major exhibitions including: *Duchamp, Man Ray, Picabia* (2008); *Cy Twombly: Cycles and Seasons* (2008); *Pop Life: Art in a Material World* (2009); *Tacita Dean: FILM, the twelfth Unilever commission for the Turbine Hall* (2011) and *Edvard Munch: The Modern Eye* (2012). He also curated contemporary group shows at Tate Modern such as *Learn to Read* (2007) and *Stutter* (2009). Cullinan spearheaded founding an acquisition committee at Tate Modern to collect modern and contemporary art from Russia, Eastern European and Central Asia. He is the author of many essays on modern and contemporary art for exhibition catalogues and articles for publications such as *Artforum*, *The Burlington Magazine*, *Frieze*, *Kaleidoscope*, *Mousse*, *October* and *Tate* etc.

ALEKSEI ALEKSANDROVICH FEDOROV-DAVYDOV

Soviet art scholar. Honored Art Worker (1960); corresponding member of the Academy of Arts of the USSR (1958). Born in Moscow, in 1900; he died in the village of Vidnoe, Moscow Oblast, in 1969. From 1919 to 1923 and between 1929 and 1934 he headed the department of modern Russian art at the Tretyakov Gallery. He taught at Moscow University from 1927 to 1931 and again from 1944 until his death; he was made head of the subdepartment of Russian and Soviet art in 1948. Between 1934 and 1944, Fedorov-Davydov taught at the Textile Institute, receiving a professorship there in 1935. He headed the research sector of the All-Union State Institute of Cinematography from 1934 to 1937 and was a professor at the institute in 1943 and 1944. Between 1948 and 1956 he headed a subdepartment at the Academy of Social Sciences attached to the Central Committee of the CPSU. Fedorov-Davydov's principal field was the history of Russian art and architecture of the 18th through early 20th centuries. He elucidated the fundamental problems in the development of Russian culture as that culture related to the life of society.

KIRILL SVETLYAKOV

Curator, head of the department of Modern Art at the State Tretyakov Gallery (since 2008). Born in Moscow, in 1976. Graduated from Moscow State University, Historical faculty (1998). DAAD scholarship (2000), Humboldt University scholarship (2000). PhD in Art History and Criticism, Curator, Art Critic. He is particularly interested in Russian and Western art of 19th and 20th centuries, modern art and museum criticism. In 2002 he discussed his theses on Paul Cezanne's realizations and the traditions of the Jack of Diamonds art group in the Soviet art during 1920-1960s. His most recent curatorship projects include: *Not Toys!?* (2009, STG), *Unbearable Freedom of Art* (2010, House of Arts at All-Russian Exhibition Center), *The Hostages of Voids* (2011, STG). Among his books two monographs on *Ilya Mashkov* (2007) and *Alexander Tyschler* (2007).

Captions and Credits

pp. 11-13 Installation view of the permanent collection of 20th century art at Tretyakov State Gallery. Photos by Arseniy Zhilyaev
p. 14 Alexey Shishiv, *Portrait of Stakhanov*, 1938, oil on canvas. Courtesy the Tretyakov State Gallery
p. 15 (top) Fedor Bogorodsky, *In memory of V.I. Lenin. Still-life*, 1932. Courtesy the Tretyakov State Gallery
p. 15 (bottom) Efim Cheptsov, *Retraining of Teachers*, 1925. Courtesy the Tretyakov State Gallery
p. 16 Victor Perelman, *Blue Blouse (Ditty)*, 1927. Courtesy the Tretyakov State Gallery
pp. 17-23 Fedor Bogorodsky, Efim Cheptsov, Victor Perelman, Arseniy Zhilyaev's collection of web images from the Russian social network Vkontakte.ru
pp. 26-39 *Museum of Proletarian Culture. The Industrialization of Bohemia*, installation views. Courtesy the artist

p. 41 Arseniy Zhilyaev, *Art Belongs to the People*, 2012, mixed media. Courtesy V-A-C Foundation
p. 43 Arseniy Zhilyaev, *Model No. 14*, 2012, mixed media. Courtesy V-A-C Foundation, Moscow
pp. 45-51 Arseniy Zhilyaev, *Collages 1980s*, 2012, mixed media. Courtesy the artist
pp. 53-55 Arseniy Zhilyaev, *Music Boxes and Home Shelves in the 1990s*, 2012, mixed media. Courtesy the artist
p. 57 Arseniy Zhilyaev, *The Hammerer*, 2012, mixed media. Courtesy the artist
p. 61 Arseniy Zhilyaev, *Screens*, 2012, mixed media. Courtesy the artist
pp. 63-64 Arseniy Zhilyaev, *Abay Wall*, 2012, mixed media. Courtesy the artist

pp. 67-79 Images from the book *Guidebook of the Experimental Complex Marxist Exposition*, Tretyakov State Gallery, Moscow 1931
pp. 80-88, Muzeon park in the vicinity of the Tretyakov State Gallery. Photos by Arseniy Zhilyaev

Reproduction, printing and binding
Grafiche Antiga, Crocetta del Montello (Treviso)
for Marsilio Editori® s.p.a. in Venice